Elder Gossett, Aug. 8, 02
Bountiful, Utah

Thank You for your interest in this book. I believe you may be enriched by its reading.
Best Wishes,
Kimball Jacobs

Faith and Fortune:

A Mormon Family In Hollywood

ISBN 1-59113-081-6

Published 2002

Manufactured in the United States of America.

Booklocker.com, Inc.
2001

Faith and Fortune:

A Mormon Family In Hollywood

By Kimball Jacobs and Shane Lester

Faith and Fortune:

A Mormon Family In Hollywood

In 1861 in a public meeting in Salt Lake City, Utah, Brigham Young stated, "If I were placed on a Cannibal island and given the duty to civilize its people, I would straightway build a theater for the purpose."

Dr. Harold I. Hansen, *A History and Influence of the Mormon Theater from 1839 –1869.* BYU, 1967.

Dedication

To my children's grandparents

Acknowledgements

My deepest gratitude to my Wee Scottish Lass, Shirley Anne, to Shane Lester, my positive driving force, to Christina R. Valentine (who proofread and typed "The First Version" many years ago), Adam Stone , John S. Schwendiamn, John D. Hawkes, Sandra Roach, Michael Richardson, Dora Flack, Robert Starling and Dreama Denver, who read the manuscript and offered valuable suggestions.

To Roger Barker for archival information.

To Mark Savage, Kimball Johnson, Ali Chamberlain, and Welster Santos whose sincere interest and encouragement meant much.

To Ray B. Jones and Harold I. Hansen; Dale M. and Sheronne Valentine and their lovely children, Mark, Ron, Melanie, Vicki, and Valerie, who were and are "Angels of Mercy."

To Aunt Thelma and their families, also my gifted and talented Thespian parents, Heber Grant and Erma Caroline Jacobs and their children, Dee, Hugh, David, and Judy and their wonderful spouses, children, and extended families.

To the many, who, along the way, by their kindness and good deeds and acts of charity have been a light and a beacon and a buoy.

Table of Contents

Chapter One

We Walked Off The Set

My two sons, Christian and Parker, had both won a part on a new television series called *Trauma Center.* It was a rare treat for me to be with my children while they worked together on the same set. Having three children all working in Hollywood at the same time was exhilarating—but taxing—on our family. My days were spent as chauffeur, acting coach, and manager. These tasks were shared with my wife Rebecca. As a mother and father we would fill our days coordinating interviews, rehearsals, casting calls, and fulfilling other ancillary tasks in an effort, as we then thought, to fulfill the dreams of our children by offering them a unique and exciting life style, a Hollywood lifestyle. For the most part my grown-up child actors do not regret, but look kindly upon their remembrances of those exceptional days when our family went to Hollywood and triumphed, to some extent, within the superficial throne and the fallacious face of Hollywood.

This small bit part on *Trauma Center* in 1983 was a stinging reminder that success in show business is temporary. Starting in 1982, all three of my four children, Rachel, Christian, and Parker were cast members on promising sitcoms. By the end of the television season in the spring of 1983, all of the sitcoms had been canceled and my children were released from their contracts. The carpet of fame and fate was pulled from underneath them without warning. From my viewpoint it would seem that three children on three separate networks could achieve some sort of longevity in the business. "Perhaps the Jacobs were not meant for that kind of fame," I mused as my two sons waited on the set of *Trauma Center,* as a complicated scene involving a simulated car accident was being coordinated and synchronized.

Christian and Parker, both veterans at the tender ages of 11 and 7 respectively, were not surprised that that day moved slowly as delay after delay impeded the on-camera filming of their particular scene. As was my nature, I enjoyed the behind-the-scenes atmosphere of the entertainment industry. It was the working class crew, the people behind the camera that seemed to be the most real and levelheaded in the industry. I cherished each opportunity to accompany my children in their work with a professional crew. It was my friendly demeanor that led me to learn new things and to meet knew people.

During the hours that we waited I struck up a conversation with the social worker and set teacher who was assigned to be on the set this day. His name was Jack Tice. According to California child labor laws, each feature film or television production where children are involved must have a social worker or set teacher present. This is a check and balance so that studios don't violate the law by keeping the child actors working excessively long hours. I learned from Mr. Tice that he was on the set of *Twilight Zone, The Movie*, during the early-morning hours of July 23, 1982, when the actor, Vic Morrow, and two Vietnamese child actors were killed in a freak accident when a helicopter crashed due to an explosion.

In 1983, criminal charges of involuntary manslaughter were filed against the director, John Landis, the production coordinator, and the pilot. The trial resulted in the acquittal for all. According to Tice, the production company didn't exactly play by the rules when it came to the labor laws concerning child actors. The night of the accident, they had conveniently sent Tice, who also wore the hat of an on-set fire fighter to the other end of the lot to keep busy. This they did, he assumed, so that he could not protest the children working so late. As a social worker, he knew the labor laws concerning child actors and would have called the Screen Actors Guild office to report the matter.

This encounter with Tice and the previous circumstance seemed fortuitous. As the hours accumulated, the delays were beginning to require my boys to break the labor laws and work beyond their allotted time. The director wanted to finish the shoot before they lost the light for the day.

I looked at my watch and counted the hours we had waited. Tice was acutely aware of the time also. When it came time for the cameras to role and my sons to finally start acting, Jack Tice took a bold and controversial stand. He announced that the production crew was in violation of labor laws and that my sons would not film today. Weighing the issue, I could have relented and let my sons do the shot. But Jack Tice was right. With this, Tice and I led my Christian and Parker away from the set. With our backs to the stunned director and crew, I began to realize the expense to the company that had hired us as well as the gravity of the situation. Tice, sensing my hesitation said, "If you let them take advantage of you, then things will never change." I anticipated a bullet in the back or at least a defaming remark such as "You'll never work in this town again!"

I was not longer naïve about "the business." Being a team player is important in Hollywood, especially for actors who are on the lower end of the food chain. Even though standing for the right principle was eternally correct, I knew this decision was going to hurt the acting prospects of my children. Our daughter Rachel later heard that the Jacobs family, while regarded as professionals and great to work with, were considered too circumspect and conservative.

Although this was not the final curtain call for my children, it was a poignant moment for me as I escorted them home. I thought then and now, back to the events and choices that brought us to Hollywood. Our lives had become a dichotomy I surmised. From the moment my wife and I decided to move our small family from the comfort and safety of Utah, to foreign, eclectic California, we were a peculiar anomaly. We were a Mormon family, founded in faith, in a religion that taught the importance of achieving a healthy and proper balance of worldly or material things, making a living from the fruits of the entertainment industry, while at the same time retaining and practicing the more enduring values of traditional Christians.

The dream that prompted us to move to Hollywood is perhaps commonly shared by others who have made the journey. But our dream was based on an optimist view of the entertainment industry. It was this dream that we felt gave us license as parents to place our jewels, our precious children, in the midst of this carnivorous business. This book has given me a space to reflect upon that dream which brought my family to Hollywood and helped me face the reality, as I openly admit, that kept me overtly passionate about the possibility that my children might achieve stardom and financial security.

Chapter Two

The Play's The Thing

For many others of this generation, the 1960s was an era of protest, revolution, and demonstration. But Brigham Young University was still a haven, an insular nexus from the turmoil that inflicted the nation. It was here that I met my future wife. Acting had brought us to college. Although arriving four years apart, I from Provo High School in 1962, and she from Bountiful High School in 1966, "fate" arranged our meeting, in none other than the Drama Department. During the BYU academic year of 1967-68, a major musical of the season, the Broadway hit, *How to Succeed in Business Without Really Trying*, cast David K. Jacobs, my older bother, as the aspiring "J. Pierpont Finch," and Rebecca as one of the "necessary-to-the-script", "scrubwomen."

Rebecca, being the on-stage and off-stage cutie that she was, caught David's attention. David, being much too old for Rebecca himself, exercised his prerogative of looking out for his little brother and introduced this gifted actress to me. I took it from there. In the words of Katherine's father from Shakespeare's *Taming of the Shrew*, "T'was a match!" Later, during our courtship, under sweltering theater lights and the smell of well-worn costumes and grease paint, we saw the possibility that the dreams of two actors could be fulfilled. It would seem that abundant circumstances shaped our lives from the centripetal forces of center stage.

On July 23, 1969, we staged our own production, a "chince" pioneer motif wedding reception with bouquets and bonnets, in the Lion House, in Salt Lake City. The Lion House was a former home and Governors Mansion of the Mormon Prophet and leader, President Brigham Young. Some of the family links to that particular location were that my great-grandmother, Zina D. Huntington Young, had once lived there as a wife of Brigham Young, rearing four motherless children and three children of her own, -one being my grandfather, Henry Chariton Jacobs.

In 1969, my rented cap and gown was returned and a milestone of study was realized. Provo and BYU became a blurred vision in the rearview mirror of our green 1960 Chevrolet Biscayne, a wedding present from Mom and Dad

Jacobs. With trailer in tow, our destination was Ririe, a small southeastern Idaho community nineteen miles from Idaho Falls. Population: 600 (more or less).

We had been hired "as a package deal." I was accepting a job as a fifth grade elementary school teacher and wrestling coach for all three-grade levels K through 12. Rebecca was hired as a teacher's aid. We soon became very involved in community theater throughout the Snake River Valley. Staying true to what we enjoyed, we became a directing as well as a performing team. Soon after our arrival in Ririe, we were put in charge of the L.D.S. Church's Ririe First Ward "road show." Beginning the following year, Rebecca would be responsible for many "road shows" as the Rigby East Stake Drama Director.

Part of our yearning of this new couple to conquer the world and to start a family was fulfilled by the birth of our first child. Early in the morning of September 26, 1970, Rebecca announced, "Kimball, it's time to go." The grueling, but exciting twelve-plus-hour labor endurance contest had officially begun at Madison Memorial Hospital in Rexburg, Idaho. The doctor was Blaine Passey, an obstetrician and quite a legend—both of his era and of the area. He was delivering about thirty babies a month!

Rebecca was having some difficulty and this delivery was excruciating. When our precious little girl emerged into the world, Doctor Passey held her up by her feet with one hand and said, "Yuck! A girl!" That was kind of typical for him and somehow he knew that that would produce a certain reaction. We witnessed firsthand that comic relief isn't confined to the theatrical stage.

During this time the drama director at the high school left and I jumped at the opportunity to add that to the other activities I was pursuing. Rachel Elizabeth Jacobs' genetic makeup contained more than a second or third generation dominant acting trait. The new Ririe High School stage and auditorium first production was Rodgers and Hammerstein's musical *Carousel.* Rachel was cast as a "babe in arms." Little Rachel was born into an energetic family engrossed in a schedule of auditions, rehearsals, and performances that didn't retard or end with her birth; but, rather, crescendoed. If Rachel weren't being taken to one of my plays, her mother was bundling her up for one of hers.

After Rebecca's duties at the elementary school were over for the day, she would get into that green Chevrolet and drive nearly twenty miles to Ricks College in Rexburg to take classes so that she could someday graduate and hold a degree. Not long after Rachel came along, Rebecca cut back on her teaching and taking classes. However, in 1971, Rebecca kept up with what was going on in the Drama Department at Ricks College and tried out for and won the lead female role in a major event of the summer theatrical season, in Jean Kerr's popular comedy *Mary, Mary.*

Rebecca soon expected the birth of our second child. Since the part was an un-pregnant female lead, appearing pregnant would not have been in the best interest of the project. So, loose-fitting clothing was the costume of the day and of the season! Rebecca's male lead opposite her in the play dropped out the last week before the show opened. Since she didn't want to kiss him on stage anyway, she convinced the director, Lyle Watson, to interview me for the part. With just a week before curtain went up, I was given the playbook with three acts to memorize. Fortunately the play "wrapped" before what was all too obvious for some became even a little bit obvious to the many who viewed the play.

Then on one of Rexburg's and the surrounding area's most blustery winter days and with an on-looking audience of 12 student nurses, a little red-headed brother named Christian made his debut, on January 11, 1972. This time Dr. Passey didn't say "Yuck"! But he did say, "Well, parents, when this little feller gets about fourteen years old, you can tell him that there were a lot of girls watching him when he was born."

Wanting to return to Utah after three years of teaching and acting in Idaho was becoming a strong impulse for Rebecca and me. It seems that in some settings both acting and teaching are by nature idealist occupations that both pay the equivalent of only "an apple a day." We were like most young couples: bound together by love and sorely tested by poverty. Wanting more for our family propelled us to look beyond the hamlet of Ririe. Before Christian was born we had been praying for our own business, such as a restaurant; something that we could call our own. About that time, Elder Boyd K. Packer, on assignment from L.D.S. Church headquarters, advised the congregation to "Be careful what you pray for. The Lord just might give it to you."

Little did we realize then how directly we would be affected by the truth of Elder Packer's words. We wanted a piece of "The American Dream". Both Rebecca and I had been trained and had worked for years in the food service industry, so the desire to have our own restaurant appeared to be a realistic goal. Risking much, our family of four left a teaching position with tenure, a friendly, wonderful little community that had assisted us in realizing many of our dreams and expectations and moved to Ogden, Utah.

We were confident, as we borrowed money from a bank, that we would succeed in the fast-food business. It was not meant to be, apparently. This became a time of inflated prices on our prime commodity: chicken! The farmers' grain prices rose so high that they would let their baby chicks die or hasten the process, so there were no mature chickens to cook and sell without paying somebody else's retail cost. As the expense rose from thirty-five cents to over a dollar twelve cents a pound, we found that this not only cut all possibility of profits, but it put the business into the dark red. This painful and costly venture lasted only about twelve months. This was a merciful end to an ambitious, but expensive, lesson in economics and business.

At the time the business failed, much of the world seemed to collapse around us. Yet, as we were just beginning to learn, defeat is often a readjustment for success. As the glass doors to what had seemed to be an opportunity for financial independence closed for good on September 11, 1973, there were bills to settle, accounts to balance, creditors to appease, and used restaurant equipment to liquidate as well as new sources of income to generate. But somehow our lives held together between odd jobs. After four moves in one year, Rebecca, Rachel, Christian and I were blessed with a darling little brick house on Darling Street, in Ogden, Utah. This was really "old stomping grounds" for me, but time would prove that not even early roots there would save us from what was about to happen.

Our new house was just two blocks away from Quincy Elementary School. And there just happened to be a fifth-sixth grade teaching position open there. After a pleasant interview with Principal Lee Gourley, the specifics were discussed and I began teaching again. As life seemed to settle down a notch, time went by and a few years later our family once again increased. The third shining star and first and only Utah-born native of the children, Parker LeGrand Jacobs, made his appearance on July 17, 1975.

Chapter Three

Saturday's Warrior

On the 7th of April, 1976, one evening, a chain of colliding events that would change our lives forever was set in motion. These events have proven to be more than just coincidence, especially by the discerning faithful who can recognize these things as "inspired of the Lord." Through Rebecca's membership and involvement with the Ogden Symphony Guild, a friend, Norma Dutson learned of an audition for Doug Stewart's and Lex de Azevedo's new Mormon musical, *Saturday's Warrior.* We had seen the play a few months previously and like many others, had been profoundly impressed! The play was different in energy and appeal, not common to any other within the genre of Mormonism.

There were openings for the part of the little girl, Emily, chorus members, dancers, and others such as the Matron. Part of the cast would be brought up from California for a spring-through-summer run. The prospect of acting in the play sounded too good to pass up. When we initially saw the performance of one of the main characters, Emily, both Rebecca and I were convinced that our oldest child, five-year Rachel, could well act the part. As parents who loved the theater, we wanted to provide this excellent opportunity for Rachel.

Hoping for the best, we left Ogden to face rush-hour traffic and made our way to the audition held at Granite School District's Highland High School in Salt Lake City. What we failed to notice was the age restrictions placed on the role of Emily. The casting director didn't want any children auditioning under the age of seven. As our hopefully unobtrusive trio waited in obscurity in the crowded auditorium, other hopeful actors and actresses, production staff, and many observers must have concluded that Rachel was not there to read for any particular part, but just "tagging along" because this Mormon mother couldn't find a baby-sitter. Rachel was five years old, but she looked much younger, perhaps even three years old.

Because the play was about a family of nine, a large number of the parts were for children. Therefore, when parents came to watch their children, from teenagers on down to age seven read for their respective parts, the congestion in the lecture –hall–style theater was threefold. There was something futile about this situation and condition. If the lights were brightened, one could view from far above and see the entire auditorium, with raised-row seating in a semicircle around the lowered stage, as lines of parents, and actors weaved and contracted like a large snake across the seating area. One might think from this high view that they were witnessing the boarding of an aircraft, or perhaps a restless crowd of faceless, nameless groupies being moved by a tide of common interest, waiting for a rock concert to begin.

Despite our valiant effort to arrive at the theater by 5:30 p.m., knowing that the audition would end at 10 p.m., the five-hour wait had inched us forward sufficiently by 10:15 p.m. to be the next to last group of eight to read. With yet a long line of actors and actresses behind us, we were told there would only be one more group to read and the group we were in could not read for a part that evening. As rarely as other than a frustrated mother can do, a protesting Rebecca spoke up out of the faceless crowd, "She's been here (pointing to Rachel) five hours. You can't send her home now. She has to read!"

Perhaps fearing a revolt from the other actors and mothers standing within ear shot of this conversation, the casting assistant capitulated and it was announced that we would be in the last group of eight to be seen. With fatigue hanging heavy in the eyes of the casting crew, we were taken with the others in the group to center stage and given the appropriate "sides" or small portions of the script to read. This was our one-time shot. Hot spotlights illuminated the stage and produced a terminating line, which carved a half-circle of light balancing on the edge of the stage, leaving the rest of the auditorium dark and mysterious.

With her mother and father personifying "the-show-must-go-on" attitude, Rachel was prompted to look past the boredom of standing around for over five hours and to do her best in reading for the part. The now courteous and somewhat captive audience was made up of other families, actresses and actors who were not going to audition that night but still waited for this last group to read. Those in attendance, still under the perception that the very young-looking Rachel was only there as a biological attachment and not as an actress, focused on the other seven actors and actresses on stage.

Rebecca and Rachel's dialogue was between the heavenly Matron and the physically unborn spirit "Emily." Rachel read her lines, speaking boldly into the darkness. Mother and daughter were only part way into the reading when

Rebecca heard a collective murmuring from the hidden crowd, and she felt that they were commenting on Rachel's reading.

Then from the darkened rotunda's seating area, an authoritative, inquiring voice rang out above the muffled whispers, "Pardon me, but is that little girl **reading** that script?" In an almost apologetic tone of not knowing why the question was asked, but wanting to give the right answer, Rachel's mother projected back into the dark, "Well . . . yes, she is."

"Thank you...You may continue."

When the dialogue ended between mother and daughter, the highly impressed, quiet crowd burst into a standing ovation, which echoed throughout the theater for this young actress. This alone could have sealed her part in the play, and the voice from the darkened tiers of seating agreed upon Rachel's merits considering all factors, excluding her age, which of course, was contrary to policy and established guidelines, according to their own criterion.

The "Voice" was that of casting director, Ben Lokey. In addition to having earned a Master's Degree in directing from the University of Utah, Ben had been a principal dancer with the Utah Ballet before it became Ballet West and was an original cast member of both the New York and Los Angeles productions of *Chorus Line*. After Rachel's reading, Ben leaned over to one of the production people and said, "I've got to have that little girl in this show!" And that he did! With unexpected surprise, Rachel took the spotlight by playing one of the primary leads, the part of Emily.

Both Rebecca and Rachel had made an impression. So much so that Rebecca was cast as one of the leads, the mother in the play. But when the producer, Lex de Azevedo, saw her, he turned that idea down because she looked too young to be the mother of seven children. (Thank you)

Ben Lokey pulled Rebecca aside and told her the news. She was very disappointed. She had always won leading roles in plays, but this time she took a step down to let Rachel have her day. Rebecca, wanting to remain with Rachel, was offered the part of being a member of the chorus. I however, had auditioned for a dancer spot but was up against some real professionals and didn't survive the cut, so I supported the two actresses in a more domestic vein.

For many, *Saturday's Warrior* had become an icon, the epitome of the "Mormon" or "L.D.S."(The Church of Jesus Christ of Latter-Day Saints) musical. One dimension of the play is the plot centering on members of a family awaiting the birth of another child, adding to their already plentiful Mormon brood. What is unusual and compelling about the story line is the parallel drama that unfolds in the pre-mortal world. This is where L.D.S. or Mormons, believe all people lived as spirit-beings before coming to earth to obtain a mortal body.

To an L.D.S. audience, the assertion that all of mankind are gathered together in this spirit existence is familiar and embracing. It is the doctrine of the Church of Jesus Christ of Latter-Day Saints that when we are born here on Earth, our memory of this pre-mortal existence is hidden from us. Through song, dance, and dialog, this stirring musical reveals a possible scenario of that existence in which all who have come to earth have shared. The play alludes to a doctrine that states that we all came to earth to obtain a body; and we are given the right of choice, an innate freedom or agency to obey and follow Jesus Christ and his teachings or to live to any other degree of spirituality we chose. The moral crux of the play asserts that our choices on earth affect the unborn lives waiting in the spirit world.

We were honored to have our child perform in a highly recognized play in Salt Lake City and then at Weber College in Ogden. However, the play had more meaning than mere recognition for us. Acting was an important dimension of our lives and the culture in which we lived

Rehearsals for *Saturday's Warrior* began in April of 1976 and the commute from Ogden to Salt Lake City became more tolerable. On one occasion during rehearsals Rebecca was talking with one of the California cast members, Cam Clark, who was playing Rachel's older brother, "Jimmy." Cam was so impressed with Rachel that he advised Rebecca, "Take her to Los Angeles. She'll never be out of work." The suggestion planted a seed for thought. It wouldn't be very long before that seed would bear fruit and Cam's comment would seem almost prophetic. Cam had a respectable amount of professional credibility even then, and went on in later years to become very busy himself in the voice-over industry, creating the voices of several of the *Ninja Turtles.*

June 11, opening night in Salt Lake City, brought a thrill, mixed with excitement and trepidation for at least two parents. Despite very active butterflies, Rachel was a natural and a smashing success. As I waited in the wings during one performance, in a tender scene in which "Emily's" (Rachel)

birth is delayed because of the choices of "Jimmy," her mortal and at times rebellious brother, Rachel was spotlighted and drew deep attention. As the ramifications of mortal choices sank into the minds of the audience, a sensitive moment carried by the spirit filled the theater as "Emily" spoke to "Jimmy" in an unseen angelic voice.

"Why didn't you keep your promise, Jimmy, why?"

As the lights dimmed, muffled sniffles could be heard from the audience. Rachel exited off stage and out of sight, winked and said, "I really made them cry that time." She was right! She was young, but absolutely in control!

That initial opportunity for Rachel to read for that part, that day, eventually unleashed a myriad of auditions and interviews, bookings and engagements, opportunities, relationships and blessings that would enrich not only her life but also the lives of her family, forever! On stage that evening, Rachel not only knew the words she was reading, but she also knew how to correctly pronounce them and how to embellish them with the correct inflections and sensitive nuances of expression. She was only five years old and read like she was a twelve-year-old. Looking young and having advanced in maturity, would prove to be our advantage in "the biz." As the production of *Saturday's Warrior* continued, the idea of going to Hollywood was met by Rebecca and me with reflective introspection.

Hollywood was a different place then, at least in our perceptions, than it is now. Today the pitfalls of Hollywood are evidenced in the products that are produced. However, Rebecca and I grew up in a different era. Indeed the movies and television of our youth, as one Hollywood insider wisely observed, "[Hollywood] used to make movies that respected [the values of the audience]." (Medved, p 90) By in large, Rebecca and I grew up with movies such as *White Christmas, Gone With the Wind, Mr. Smith Goes to Washington, Stagecoach, Wuthering Heights* and so on. These movies "demonstrate that it is possible to create entertainment of enduring worth without assaulting the fundamental values of people." (Medved, p 343)

For us the choice to go to Hollywood was balanced with our optimism and our preconceived notions about the film and television industry, and of course, the inherent religious beginnings of drama itself.

Chapter Four

The Mailbox

Saturday's Warrior kept mother and daughter and everybody else busy for the summer. As curtains rose and descended night after night, Rebecca and I became restless with what seemed to be our intended lot. With the cascade of successes and defeats revolving in our minds, the idea of going to Hollywood, although a shift in paradigm, looked like an avenue for fulfillment. The hope for success and the lack of permanent stability in our present location made the ideal of "Hollywood" seem very appealing. After all, what more could we lose?

While mother and daughter continued to perform and I played the part of "Mr. Mom" at home, some important events were leading to an impending decision.

During this period of time I had once again left the walls of the classroom that fall of 1976 and searched for success in the business community. Among other things, I began to work at a food storage company. Then an opportunity to go to California presented itself. From the first through the fifth of September, my son Christian and I attended the International Association of Cancer Victims and Friends' three-day convention at the Los Angeles Marriott Hotel. On the schedule at the convention was an impressive list of guest speakers, such as Paavo Airola, Dr. John Christopher, Gloria Swanson and other world-renowned authorities in the arts of healing by natural means.

Alternative medicine had become an interest for us since the summer of 1974, when it was discovered that Rebecca's symptoms of slurred speech, tingling and numb fingertips, spots before the eyes, and general weakness and lethargy indicated the condition of hypoglycemia. We began studying all we could find, first about the blood-sugar-adrenaline relationships, and what affected them specifically, and then more on the broader and general topic of achieving and maintaining optimum good health. This interest, unknown to us at the time, would bring us closer to moving to Hollywood.

Something somewhat magical and indescribable happened when Christian and I arrived in California for the convention. When Christian saw the Pacific Ocean and then got to take his shoes off and venture out into it, it was as if two great forces of the universe came together in a moment of profound fulfillment of some sort of destiny.

When the convention was over, we went back to Utah with some very important contacts. One name that I came across while in the Santa Monica area was that of a commercial and theatrical agent for children, Mary Grady. This information later proved to be invaluable.

One beautiful Utah October day, the telephone rang. It was Uncle David Jacobs. His message was two-fold: First, David was directing and casting talent for a short movie that he was producing. From various family get-togethers, where Rachel had preformed a song or a poem for the group, he was impressed so much that he rewrote the screenplay to include his vivacious and precious little niece. David wondered if Rachel would be interested in acting in his movie, and would her parents give their permission?

"OF COURSE!"

The short movie, called *The Mailbox*, was about an elderly lady whose primary contact with her family was by letter and how important those letters and other neighbor relationships were to her! The message was to "never forget grandparents or the lonely or elderly when you can write them letters to cheer them up." David rewrote the story and cut out a part in which the elderly widow spoke to a bird. This bird was replaced with Rachel, making the character of the old woman more approachable and endearing. In a few months Rachel would play the role of the little neighbor girl who developed a strong relationship with a truly loving elderly lady, whose real name was "Lethe." The movie went on to win the Cine-Gold Eagle Award and garnered high acclaim from The Postal Carriers of America, for whom it was presented at their national convention at Bryce Canyon, Utah in 1977. It won other top educational and industrial awards and honors and was entered in the 1977 Annual Academy of Motion Picture Arts and Sciences Oscar Awards competition for the short subject live action category and was one of the surviving 15 finalists of the many hundreds of films submitted.

Uncle David's second message was that auditions for *The New Mickey Mouse Club* Mouseketeers were being held in Burbank, California, in the next few weeks. Would Rachel's parents be interested in Rachel's auditioning? Through a close friend, Uncle David could set up an audition time with the producer Michael Wuergler. "OF COURSE!" The big problem with such limited funds was "how?" Several days later, Rebecca had the exact information on the audition day and time and everything was set, everything except how to swing the finances for the plane flight for Rachel and her mom. With my new job in food storage providing little income, the prospect of affording plane tickets seemed nil.

The frustration was further compounded when Rebecca received money from her grandfather, Elder LeGrand Richards, a member of the Quorum of the Twelve Apostles of The Church of Jesus Christ of Latter-Day Saints. The money, which was just about the right amount to purchase plane tickets to Burbank, was given as a gift to be put into a missionary fund for Christian and Parker. Rebecca struggled with the ethics of the situation: should she use the money to fly to the audition, or leave it for its intended use? Finally they decided to keep the money for which it was intended and let the audition, opportunity go.

In the short-term perspective, perhaps one of the biggest mistakes we would ever make was to miss that audition. Instead of giving up so quickly and thinking there was no one in their lives who had $120 to lend on a short-term basis, it may have been better to have done a little asking, begging if necessary. Two years later, Michael Wuergler actually saw Rachel in a church production, and in a conversation with Rebecca, he discovered that Rachel was previously scheduled for the Mouseketeers' audition. Michael said, "I'm just sick. Why weren't you there? I would have used her!" Who knows, things could have been a little better, a little sooner, for a lot longer!

Some weeks before, in October of 1976, on the advice of a friend, Rebecca had taken Rachel to the Hilton Hotel in Salt Lake City to meet with the most prominent acting and modeling agent in Utah, Susan McCarty. Cards with information such as telephone number, age, and address were filled out and pictures left. Later that month, Susan McCarty called about an audition for Rachel in a Utah Power and Light television commercial. There seemed to be dozens of other little girls and boys at the audition, so it was with much anticipation that the family waited for further word.

There was celebration at our home when the McCarty Agency called back on November 30 with a commercial job. What happened next was a typical tactic of the entertainment industry. The casting director picked 20 children and brought them all together on the day of the shoot. The task then was to find the most out-spoken child. Despite this hidden agenda, Rachel was not the most obnoxious or loud. She was simply, consistently obedient. The commercial required the little lead actor or actress to be strictly exact and concise.

The commercial was called *The Oven Pepper.* The gist of the commercial was a group of children where gathering around the oven door, peeking in it to see if the cupcakes were done. Rachel had the assignment of opening the door each time. Repeatedly the oven was opened until finally the cupcakes were done, to the delight of the children! The filming occurred in one day, as was typical in the industry, especially when so many people were to be involved, particularly children. The scene had to be rehearsed and rehearsed and then shot over and over until everything was in sync and was the best product possible. This was a departure from the dynamics of the theater, which was the only frame of reference in acting that Rachel had at the time. In the theater one rehearses rigorously, but when it's time to perform, what one does is what one gets. In a commercial, despite the final editing touches, video, lights, sound, set, and picture must not only be orchestrated in harmony to produce a finished product, but everything—especially in this particular *The Over Pepper* spot—everything was what is in the business called “tight, tight, tight.”

After a painfully long day of shooting under hot lights, one of the production people said, "That little girl must have opened that oven door a hundred times.” Rachel, standing nearby, overheard the comment and corrected the conversation in a kind and childlike way, wisely retorting, "One hundred forty!" She had been counting! The people from the Stockdale Corporation, the ad agency in charge of the commercial, called Rachel "incredible" because "she was so patient to work with under such uncomfortable conditions for such a long time without ever complaining." And at her age she was incredible.

One August, Rebecca and I put a “House for Sale” sign in our front yard. It was sold by that same evening. We took what little equity we had gained in two years and moved three miles away into an upstairs, two-bedroom apartment. This was somewhat of a challenge after living in our own home. I made a telephone call to what I hoped was the same reputable children's agent in Los Angeles, Mary Grady that I had heard about while in California with Christian in September.

She came right on the phone and was typically vivacious and personable! After being asked if she would represent Rachel as her agent, and what to do for that to happen, Mary said that she wanted to meet Rachel. Mary asked where we lived.

"Utah" was the reply.

"Where... Utah?" she asked.

"Yes" I replied.

After a very long "well-l-l-l..." Mary said, "Could you send a few pictures of Rachel, some that don't ever need to be returned, along with birth date and telephone number. That would be a good start." Then she added, "Oh, and by the way, it would be best to be living in the Los Angeles area!"

Mary was precisely correct. Because of very short notifications for most interviews and auditions, Utah would just be too far to travel each day or even two or three times a week. Timing was one consideration; cost was the biggest problem. With this information left to consider, Rebecca and I saw the hopes of going to Hollywood as still improbable, impractical, and even scary!

On the morning of December 7, 1976, I opted not to stay with what I felt was the very slow-moving food storage company. I then began the task of trying to collect the money due me and to find a new job. As I turned to the classified section of the Ogden Standard Examiner, a small ad jumped right off the page at me: "Going on I-15 to Long Beach. Will take your personal belongings. Need rider to defray cost." As the number was dialed and the "hello" delivered, the voice on the other end questioned, "Is this you, Kim?" It happened to be Pat Hardy, one of our former neighbors from Harrisville, in northwest Ogden. Details about the truck were that it would be available to be loaded at 6 that evening, and they wanted to leave at 3 a.m. the next morning.

Major decision! This was a big one! After collecting the children together, we explained the situation. "We have a big decision to make here, kids, were thinking of moving to California. Do you think you might like that? Remember, Christian, last month when you went swimming in the ocean? That was California!" Christian was immediately interested. Rachel and Parker had quizzical expressions as they looked up at the two adults, not fully understanding the gravity of the situation. We knelt down and asked our Heavenly Father to help us know what to do. It actually took most of the day to arrive at the decision. But when the answer came, we sensed an urgency to get everything packed and loaded. Our lives were about to change most dramatically!

After loading the 16-foot paneled truck, I drove it to Harrisville, climbed into the back, was locked in, and off we went. The temperature was in the low 30s that morning, but it was a bit warmer inside the cab of the truck. With Keith driving, about one hour later, at a fuel stop in Provo, the Hardys took pity and compassion on their stow-a-way and invited me to ride in the cab with them, which I appreciated.

Because some rather delicate items had not been packed with proper protection, Keith had to keep the speed down. We three travelers pulled into San Bernadino in about fifteen hours from start time. While pit-stop procedures were being carried out, I hurried to a pay phone and dialed my Aunt Wilma and Uncle Tom Broadbent of Riverside.

"You're where? . . . San Bernardino? . . . You want to what? . . . Put a truckload of furniture and things in our garage?"

"Yes, Uncle Tom, would that be all right?"

"Kimball, it's a good thing you called when you did. Your Aunt Wilma and I were just on our way out the door for the evening. We'll wait here for you." Arriving in California without a place to stay may be seen as foolish or perhaps faithful luck. I had never been to the Broadbents' house, but somehow we got there quickly, unloaded, and the Hardys were on their way to Long Beach.

As Wilma and Tom left for their appointment, the warm air of Southern California sent a synthesizing wariness through my body as I recalled the winter conditions of December in Utah. We stopped at the gas station in San Bernardino, and I remembered seeing people walking about in short selves. It was December and I had just come from an ice box. Now came the monumental task of finding a job and a place for my family to live. We were coming to Hollywood! Not only would faith get us there, but it would take a determined, pioneer grit to keep us there!

Chapter Five

The Agent

Being the gracious people that they were, the Broadbents permitted me their solo, and somewhat displaced nephew, a place to stay for a few days. To aid my search for a new job and accommodations for my family, they supplied their new compact foreign import automobile. Not wanting to impose, I looked for other lodging immediately. Our other relatives living in California, The Callisters, had invited us to "stay over" if we were ever in the area. I thought I would take them up on the offer and they were contacted. They kindly responded, and I then stayed with them.

The Callister home sat perched atop a lovely high Glendale hill overlooking the San Fernando Valley from the east. From that vantage point, I studied the freeway maps and "the lay of the land" and determined that, all factors being considered, the North Hollywood area would be the most logical place to begin. As I went from one apartment complex to another in that North Hollywood area for the next nine days, I heard something very reminiscent of an old broken (scratched) record, "Two children are okay, but not three. Sorry." Excuse after excuse, over and over again, day in, day out, "no room at the inn."

On my second week with the Callisters, I was able to secure a job in the North Hollywood/Van Nuys area that paid minimum wage and was in the food service industry, preparing meals at a convalescent center. This was a start.

While staying at the Callisters', I contacted some professional actors, such as Gordon Jump and Nathan and Ruth Hale. When asked what he thought about moving the family from Utah with the intention of going into "Show Biz," Gordon Jump (with credits such as "*W.K.R.P. in Cincinnati* and most recently, the *Maytag Man*) responded, "I did it. Give it a try for a year and then you'll know better." The Hale Family had operated the very successful Glendale Center Theater for more than thirty years. Surely they would have a good feel for what to do. Ruth responded, "I have these beautiful and talented daughters." (Knowing the family personally, I knew that she was not exaggerating.) "They are good actresses. I've taken them for over a hundred interviews and auditions for films and television commercials, and they have landed not one. . . . You'll never know if you don't try, but that has been our experience. . . . They either seem to be too blonde or too dark or too thin or too fat, too tall or too short. It's hard to out-guess what the casting agents really want."

Meanwhile, back in Utah, Rebecca was busily packing everything she could, arranging and setting things up for the family. Fortunately, there were family like Mom and Dad Jacobs and neighbors and former neighbors, some of whom were "just happening by," who pitched in mightily and offered tremendous help to the effort. One such person was Ralph Johnson of Ogden, who, when Rebecca asked, "How can we ever repay you?" responded, "Just help someone else when you can."

As the family occupied two locations, the time came to film *The Mailbox.* Cameras rolled at the Brigham Young University Motion Picture Studios in Provo and at Lethe Tadje's Swiss architectured home in the pristine "village" of Midway. Filming went well. The next several days Rebecca collected money, a partial month's rent, and deposits were returned and the food storage company came through with a survivable amount. The trailer hitch for the U-Haul was miraculously located and put on the car for the best possible price. Once again there was another day of *Mailbox* filming on location. Then, until snow fell for the outside shots, the project was put on hold.

Rebecca stopped by BYU to check the “ride board” and contacted a Jeannette Herzog, who was looking for transportation to California. The idea was to have a riding companion and trade-off driver for Rebecca. Jeannette was from Aarburg, Switzerland. Being a savvy traveler making her way across the United States, she was a great help to the somewhat apprehensive and careful Rebecca.

On Tuesday, December 12, just before the family pulled out, the phone rang. I was calling from California. Arrangements as to where and when to meet were made, and off the family drove into a rather frosty winter's night headed southwest. Just outside Provo, the three children finally fell asleep, leaving Rebecca and Jeannette to visit and to get to know each other better. About 1:30 in the morning, the headlights began to dim. After pulling over to the side of the road, the car completely died. Rebecca took a long, lonely look at the dark, desolate surroundings. There hadn't been much traffic coming or going for some time. The night's chill began to creep into and through the protective layers of the automobile.

When small faint headlights appeared in the rearview mirror, it seemed like the only hope on this frozen desolate desert of Southwestern Utah. After being flagged down by Jeannette, the vehicle stopped. The approaching vehicle, which now could be discerned by Rebecca and Jeannette as a truck, had passed them and then slowed to a halt some distance beyond. They saw the glowing lights, then heard a sort of groaning sound as transmission gears unmeshed and remeshed. The truck was occupied by three men. The men seemed leery as Rebecca explained their situation. Rebecca felt equally leery of the men at first. The three men were coming home from an L.D.S. Church basketball game and said that they didn't have a chain or tow cables with them, but they would go into the nearest town where they lived, fifteen miles ahead, and would return as soon as possible.

As taillights disappeared into the blackness, the trek to California didn't seem so inviting for Rebecca. It began to get uncomfortably cold as they waited and waited. The children were still asleep and bundled up. Again headlights appeared in the rearview mirror. This time a car slowed down as it passed them and then pulled off the road several hundred yards away. This made Rebecca somewhat nervous, and silent prayers were offered. Finally, just as the car began to back up toward them, there came the three men again, in the same truck, which they hooked onto the Ford Pinto station wagon. Seeing this, the car in front pulled away.

The nearest town was Beaver. One of the men suggested his father-in-law's motel would be a suitable place for Rebecca, Jeannette, and the children to spend the night. The California-bound travelers were put up for the night. The next morning, thanks to the advice of the three men from the night before, the least expensive and most honest repair shop in town was found. The regulator replacement was only $25 and the group was back on their way by 9 a.m. The anonymity of two of the three men is still a mystery, but the leader was former BYU basketball player of the late 1960s and early 1970s, Lynn Kay Parsons! Grateful and eager travelers made their way to Las Vegas and contacted me to let me know of their delay.

Later, just outside San Bernardino, the Pinto ran completely out of gas and stopped right there on the freeway! Thank goodness for Jeannette! After dodging cars and climbing over a freeway fence, a small gas can, large enough to contain sufficient fuel to reach to the nearest gas station, was obtained. It was there that they called me. When they all arrived in San Bernadino, how relieved everyone felt! We returned Tom and Wilma's car to Riverside, stopped in for a short time for visiting, and started off on the last, but what felt like the longest, leg of the journey. Would Los Angeles and North Hollywood ever appear? Finally, our little family ended up checking into a local motel on Lankershim Boulevard at 2 a.m. on December 14, 1976.

As with many in a strange, new place, commonality promotes the best contacts and the best results. While I was at work at the convalescent center in Van Nuys, Rebecca went over to an L.D.S. Church building. Someone was there to let her into the building, where she made several calls. The L.D.S. Stake President's wife, Katherine Barton, gave Rebecca a referral of someone she knew who managed an apartment, a Betty Bacon.

Rebecca contacted Betty and learned good news! An apartment would be available in three to four days, just as soon as it was painted and cleaned. Rebecca went right over to Betty's, paid the last of her money for the month plus the deposit and key fee. Rebecca looked at the two-bedroom, upstairs place and, even though it was filthy, asked to be able to move into it the next day around noon. That was agreeable with Betty. Things were starting to go well.

Desperation, out of necessity, often brings people closer to the Lord, relying upon his mercies. This was especially true for our family; being tossed into a foreign environment with few family members and no other friends, our small Mormon family relied on our Heavenly Father to see us through this difficult situation. Even though the apartment had electricity, the natural gas had been shut off and not turned back on, and wouldn't be until the following week. So, nothing but cold water was available without borrowing some from the neighbors. That evening we slept in sleeping bags on our apartment floor and were grateful, very grateful, for the roof over our heads.

On our first Saturday in town, we drove back out to Riverside to Aunt Wilma's and Uncle Tom's to pick up more of our things. This became a regular procedure for several weeks until everything that belonged to us was moved out of the Broadbent's garage.

It was now seven days before Christmas. What could be termed as a "fickle flight to California" by family and friends, had left us depleted of funds. With substantial bills and only the reality that I would be starting a new job in south Los Angeles for a furniture manufacturing and drapery company, the situation looked extremely bleak for our first Christmas in this snow-less climate. For

Monday's Family Home Evening, Rebecca and I announced to the children that with money being as scarce as it was, the family could either go miniature golfing for a family activity or buy a Christmas tree, but not both. Miniature golf won out.

It was our lifelong practice and belief to return to the Lord at least a tenth part of "our increase," or profit from employment. We had a very strong conviction of this principle in our lives. There were always many things we couldn't afford, we made sure that the Lord was paid first; quite miraculously everyone else ended up getting paid too. This was a constant trend for us: to expect the unexpected. So it was, when "out of the blue" came a most welcomed, albeit unexpected check, which would really bless our lives.

The problem was, we had not been in town even a week and had not established residency. On Wednesday, December 20, Rebecca was looking for a bank at which to cash the check we had received from out of state. Because we had no phone in our apartment, Rebecca went to the L.D.S. Stake Center, hoping to use a phone once again. The building was locked, but some youths conducting a car wash at the church gave her approximate directions and told her about how far down the street to go to find the phone. Rebecca drove down Vineland Avenue until she came to what she thought was the building the youth had described.

The traffic was so swift flowing at that intersection, she could not pull over quickly enough to turn in at the United California Bank. As she passed through the intersection she noticed another building, the North Hollywood Federal Savings and Loan Association building. She parked and went in. While in the bank she fell into the ranks of the proverbial wait-in-line routine. As she was waiting, she broke protocol and for some reason gravitated toward a certain teller. So strong was this feeling to Rebecca, she even gave up her otherwise favorable position to be helped by this certain teller. These actions didn't seem odd at the time, just as a small whisper of inclination. When her turn to be helped finally arrived, identification was requested. As Rebecca reached into her wallet for her I.D., the McCarty Agency card fell out. The woman bank teller, who was unusually friendly, noticed the card. She then asked if Rebecca was interested in that kind of service, because, she added, "We have that kind of agent upstairs."

Rebecca said, "No, thank you. We already have an agent we have written to from Utah." The woman asked, "What's her name?"

“Mary Grady."

“That's who's upstairs," The woman replied.

Immediately, Rebecca left the counter and went upstairs to the fifth floor. Up until this time, with the pressure and stress of moving and filming in Utah, we hadn't contacted the agent in California. In Mary Grady's office they were in the midst of Christmas celebrations. The mood was open and festive; Rebecca was not blocked by traditional secretarial interference. She poked her head through the door of Mary's office and introduced herself.

Although somewhat surprised, Mary was more than affable and admitted the pictures that we had sent to her of Rachel “must have been ... misplaced.” Mary then said she needed someone that afternoon to audition for a *Jack-in-the-Box* commercial, a small blonde. She asked, "Is Rachel small?"

“Yes!"

“Go home and get her!"

Rebecca raced back to the apartment to pick up Rachel, Christian, and Parker. She found Parker covered in mom's lipstick, not the subdued shade, the bright stuff. Without time to solve this problem, she rounded the children up and off they went back to Mary Grady's. We naturally assumed that now blonde-headed Christian could have as much success as Rachel, and the plan was to get him and his brother Parker into the industry too.

Rachel's memory of this event centers around the Christmas wreath on the front office door of Mary Grady’s office. It was lavishly and colorfully decorated with candy canes hanging down low by red satin ribbon. Alongside the wreath was a pair of scissors attached by a string, thus offering a holiday treat to clients, most of whom were children. Christian remembers vividly going into Mary Grady's office and reading for the first time. For a child, this situation is a time "to be good" and "be on your best behavior." As we waited, Rebecca was cleaning their faces and attempting to clean the red lipstick faced Parker, admonishing every one, "OK, we've got a big thing in here, guys. Let's be good."

“It wasn't that big of a deal to us," Christian recalls. "We didn't even know what was going on." After having Christian and Rachel read, Mary said, looking at Parker, "I love this baby, I want this baby. I'll represent all three of your children." Then turning specifically to Rachel, but directing her comment to Rebecca, Mary said, "Someone must have sent her special."

Rebecca replied, "Someone did."

With the address received from Mary, we were on their way to our first "big-time interview," but our car was almost out of gas. The only form of money we had was that two-party, out-of-state check. Now with me, we went to the bank across the street from Mary Grady's office. The teller absolutely refused to service my request and gave specific details, two or three times at least, of what the institution’s policy on such matters were. Looking around, I saw a very clean-cut, middle-aged gentleman who appeared to be someone of some importance in the organization. I introduced myself and explained the check problem.

“You’re from Utah?” the well-groomed, mild mannered gentleman inquired.

“Yes,” I replied. Whereupon the man said he knew someone from Utah, a Chris Toronto, a neighbor, originally from Spanish Fork, Utah.

“Chris and his sisters, Maria, Elizabeth and Joan, and my brother and sister and I all went to school at BYU together," I said. After comparing memories, the man said, "Where's your check?" He okayed it on the spot, and off we drove.

The Jack-in-the-Box interview was our first real professional opportunity in the "The Big City" and feeling blessed, we humbly expected that Rachel would get the job.

At this first "Hollywood" audition, Rebecca noticed that one of the other little girls there had a beautiful photograph of herself. Rebecca asked her mother, who had taken the picture?

“Bob Whiteman."

We later asked Mary Grady about Mr. Whiteman. Arrangements were made and we became acquainted with Mr. Whiteman, an excellent photographer who has since passed away. He took many, many actor's pictures, including Rachel's and Christian's first ones in the big city, and he came all the way from Oregon to do it.

Although that first interview did not result in a job, it was an important learning experience and an adventure. Our family was not discouraged by this initial rejection, but it prompted us to sit-up and take note of the difficulty of the task at hand. In "The Industry"—entertainment, acting, commercials, movies, print work, voice-over and so forth—the average ratio of "strike it" job offers per interviews or auditions was, at that time, one per nineteen for children or minors. For adults the ratio is much more lopsided, sometimes into the hundreds. That was one of the first questions we asked Mary Grady. Unknown to the hopeful family, Rachel's first break would come nearly four months later.

One of the first tasks to accomplish when attempting to get your children into the advertising and entertainment industry is to get some good pictures. When the offer was made by Mary Grady to represent all three children, the cost of pictures was excessive on our limited budget. About this time, Dick Woody from Mary Grady's office called. He must have been reviewing some paperwork in the office and thought he had detected an error.

“Mary makes it a policy to only represent one member from a family." Dick said,

Rebecca replied, "I'm sorry, but I've already got pictures taken of my children, and besides, Mary said she would take all three."

A short pause, then Dick said, "Wait a minute and I'll talk with Mary.” He then came back on the phone. "Okay, Mary said it was okay.”

It was now Christmas Eve and because of the miniature golf extravaganza, there was no tree in our little apartment. There were, however, some green garbage can liners and some scissors that were used to cut the liner into the shape of an evergreen tree. There was tape that fastened the liner to the wall. When the children colored some paper ornaments and cut them out and stuck them to the liner; it was one of the most beautiful Christmas trees our family had ever seen. Love and happiness bloomed in that little apartment, and that made all the difference!

A few minutes after the last ornaments on the makeshift tree were taped, the doorbell rang. Who was it? We certainly weren't expecting anyone. When we opened the door, there was only a gigantic wrapped present the size of a refrigerator box with a beautiful bow, with no one in sight. We dragged the big, heavy present into our living room and decided to open it right then. Inside that big box were many presents, all beautifully wrapped! Not all the presents were opened that night, but those that were opened were very special. There seemed to be something for everybody. Someone knew that there was a baby Parker and a four year-old boy and a five year-old girl and a mom and a dad! What a great Christmas Eve to remember! "Silent Night" was sung, family prayer was observed, and so much was right with our world!

Chapter Six

Skeets

When the Holiday season passed, our family still had to meet the realities of daily living. The naive, unwritten agenda for the family was to survive through the medium of acting for all available members of the family. Also, Rebecca and I had discussed the possibility of my returning to college while in California to become a chiropractor and ultimately a naturopathic physician. Meanwhile, it was determined that working construction and other odd jobs for me would be the rule until our financial situation became more providential.

Some of the adjustments to North Hollywood were of a cultural nature. The thin spread of diversity within the cultures represented in Utah and Idaho hardly compared to our experiences in California. But more of a shift in paradigm to us was the xenophobic life-styles of our neighbors. We were used to cohesive neighborhoods where neighbors knew not only next-door neighbors, but everyone else on the street and in the general community four and five blocks on all sides. But not so in North Hollywood. It was as different as literally living in a foreign country within a few hundred yards of the apartment.

Although smog was a new and accepted reality for us as displaced Utahans, the climatic milieu was more intriguing. The lack of seasonal changes was a pleasant adjustment. The loss of the sweet smell of lilacs and iris and peonies were replaced by gardenia, and flowering citrus trees; the orange, lemon, tangerine, and the banana plant, and magnolia and eucalyptus trees. Compared to the harsh climate of Utah, this initially seemed, if not like the Garden of Eden, then at least a fascinating flip-side to Utah.

We had come to California with goals and expectations. Education was very important to us and an ad in one of the local papers had caught our eye since our arrival in North Hollywood. It advertised a private, Carden Method school. A woman named Mae Carden had begun a number of schools across the country and one of them just happened to be starting up in the North Hollywood area. Knowing something of the reputation of the school, we wished that our children might attend. However, we both put the idea in the back of our minds until our basic needs could be managed.

As Rebecca was browsing about in a large department store in town, she overheard a women in conversation about the Carden-Lee School being started in North Hollywood. Rebecca introduced herself to this woman who turned out to be Phyllis McDowell, the director of the new Carden-Lee School in Sun Valley near North Hollywood. As a result, Rachel became the fourth and Christian the fifth student of that school. This story may be disturbing to all husbands, as it can be deduced: Rebecca was "**Inspired**" to go shopping.

We felt that our children were very capable of going as far up the ladder to stardom and success as anyone had ever gone. That expectation—that the children were good, "very good"—was a driving force in our coming to and staying in California. Feeling so strongly about our children, we did not want that talent to be wasted or to go undeveloped. Also, while in Hollywood, Rebecca and I had hoped that our acting careers might take off. We expected that acting jobs could be a supplementary part of our income and out of this necessity we always updated our records with American Federation of Television and Radio Artist, and kept a keen eye out for an opportunity for us to join S.A.G., the principle union for actors. We updated resumes and pictures and remained on the lookout for acting possibilities. However, it became apparent that the children had more "action" than did their parents.

While staying with Norinne and Reed Callister, before the rest of the family moved from Utah, I was helped by Reed to find a job. A friend of the Callisters', Les Young, was looking for help, and after an interview, I was hired. The job was at a furniture manufacturing company located in Compton, near Watts in South Los Angeles. After the family arrived with only one car, which was reserved for Rebecca to take to interviews, I was left to the mercy of mass transit, via the bus system. My day began at 4:30 a.m. After a 3-to 12-block walk or run to a bus stop, I was on my way to Compton. After several transfers, I would arrive at work at 7 am. This was no easy adjustment from the stable ebb and flow of traffic in the Utah and Idaho region and the accessibility of living close to one's work.

One morning, on my way to work there were four teenagers on the bus sitting in front of me. It was against the law to smoke on the bus; however, these young men didn't seem to care much for that particular law. As they were smoking, a scent, a pungent, sweet smell that was unfamiliar to my senses slithered its way back to my location. It was a stop or two before my curiosity and naivety got the best of me. "Hey, guys," I queried, "is that marijuana you're smoking? I've never smelled it before!"

In dead silence, dumbfounded at this intrusion of their invisible air space, the youths gave me a united, albeit deadly stare. I had expected at least some sort of nod of the head or blink of the eye or even some word or phrase of acknowledgment. Instead, they stared at me glassy-eyed, which I translated into mental words, "Yeah, now we'll have to kill yugh!" Convinced that I had read their minds correctly, I promptly exited the bus at the next stop. I made it to work and back again that evening to live another day.

My boss, Mr. Young, was so concerned about my general safety, although unaware of the bus incident; he occasionally dropped me off near a bus stop not far from our apartment. Since Les lived in Tarzana, it was on his way. I lived near the Ventura freeway and Vineland Avenue bus stop. The situation was convenient for both parties and much appreciated by me.

On one occasion when Les Young drove me home, he asked me in a serious voice, " Reed Callister's father-in-law is a high-ranking member within his church. Are you acquainted with the man?"

Being careful and suspecting something loaded coming my way, I replied, "Are you speaking of Elder LeGrand Richards?"

"Yes." said Les, "What does he do?"

"Do you mean for a living or what he does in the Church?"

Beginning to sound a bit abrupt, Les answered, "In the church, for the Mormon Church, what does he do?"

Now I replied more enthusiastically, "Of course you know that the term "Mormon" is just a nickname for the church that Reed and Norinne and their family belong to. The real name is The Church of Jesus Christ of Latter-Day Saints, and Elder Richards goes all over the world representing the Church in an administrative capacity, establishing new units of the Church called stakes, wards, and branches and makes changes within these organizations, such as leadership positions. And he gives speeches and meets with members and non-members of the church."

I felt a little relieved after having said such a mouthful, in almost one nervous breath and I almost started to relax a bit when Les said in a tone that carried with it a flavor of annoyance, "Isn't there something else he does?"

“Yes", I said, having intentionally held back on extra information, not wanting to impose my religious beliefs upon or offend my Jewish boss.

“Go ahead, Kimball, hit me, hit me," I could almost hear Mr. Young saying. Okay, so I hit him with what an Apostle of the Lord does and is.

“Elder Richards is a special witness to all the world that Jesus is the Christ, the Messiah, the Son of the Living God," I concluded and then both driver and passenger slipped into profound silence!

As I spoke these last words, I prayed that my reply was adequate. Before another word would be spoken, the bus stop came into view and it was the end of the ride for me. I thanked my boss and stepped out of his shinny metallic Mercedes, pondering the event that just transpired. I also wondered if I would have a job the next morning, but I was grateful for the opportunity to have stood for Christ and to have born witness of Him.

After having the soul-refining experience of working in Compton, I hung up my broom and gave notice to Les Young on the second week of January, a Wednesday. I then submitted an application for general work at the San Fernando Valley's LDS Employment center on Thursday. The next day I heard from Mr. Am Smart that a Dean Moser was looking for someone to help in the office at the distribution department of the Doty-Dayton Film Corporation. These are the people who produced the movie *Where the Red Fern Grows.* The company was located in the same building as the bank where earlier we were able to cash our out-of-state check. In fact, the company was so large, it occupied the entire fourth floor of that building. This was in some critical ways, a huge negative cash-flow factor, as the company and I would soon experience.

With no real acting break in Hollywood for any member of the family at that time, we could have easily been discouraged and wanting to return to the security of the mountains of Utah. Determined that we had made the right choice, we stood our ground.

A telephone call with the news that filming would resume immediately on Uncle David's movie was very welcome. In the first week of February 1977,

Rachel, Rebecca, and I left North Hollywood for Utah to complete *The Mailbox* filming. The filming went well, and we were soon back on the trail to California.

On February 19, 1977, I wrote in the family journal:

> I had determined to pay tithing on $100 my father gave me while in Utah, also for a check from Doty-Dayton for $110. I didn't have enough to pay our $225 rent for the month. Today, Saturday, a letter came from the new owner of our apartment. The letter said that since we moved in on the middle of the month, but had paid full rent, this month would be the adjusting month for the correct payment and we pay only one-half the rent.

There were many times when we felt the indication of the unseen powers at work on our behalf. One such happening took place at what was then called Anderson Graphics on Woodman Avenue in Van Nuys, just west of North Hollywood. That was the place where proof sheets and /or photo negatives were taken to be reproduced into the actual headshot and composite pictures, which are absolutely necessary for interviews.

Being new in town, we felt that our daughter wasn't perhaps the only Rachel Jacobs in the business. And we were right! In fact, we fully expected that we might have to use a different stage name for Rachel. Our feelings were confirmed when we went to Anderson Graphics to pick up our pictures, and they gave us the pictures of another "Rachel Jacobs."

This concerned us somewhat; we hoped that we might be first at the Screen Actor's Guild to register our Rachel Jacobs before the other "Rachel Jacobs." Everything is in the name. If we were second, we would have to change Rachel's name or get out of the business. When joining a guild, your name becomes exclusive. Joining the Screen Actor's Guild was mandatory. In "Right-to-Work-States," such as Utah, union membership is optional, but in California, you must be in a union to work.

Some weeks later Rebecca was at the guild office after receiving official notice from the guild that the Rachel Jacobs from Utah had permission to register at the guild under that very name "Rachel Jacobs." She then received an interesting explanation of what had happened. The other Rachel Jacobs' application had arrived on the guild office desk first, but had been buried in a stack of other applications and paperwork. When the application for Rachel Jacobs from Utah came in, it was processed first.

After the name issue was settled, in order for Rachel to act within the Screen Actors Guild in California, she also had to have a work permit. After the application was approved at the Department of Labor Standards Enforcement in downtown Los Angeles, it was sent back to the applicant to be presented when the minor arrived on set for work and passed into the hands of "The Set Teacher."

The set teacher kept track of the hours the minor child was "in school" on set, and there were also ratings or grades given in the various subjects. Ideally, the minor child's home school and home school teacher(s) worked in concert with the child's shooting schedule and prepared curriculum accordingly to cover the one or two days, or one of two weeks, or an entire school season away from the regular classroom.

Although we got hot on the trail of jobs, after attending numerous interviews, we had momentary success when Christian was able to do some print jobs (modeling in magazines and catalogs). With a few solid acting experiences now under Rachel's belt, she was more than ready for acting jobs in Hollywood. Finally she got her chance. After the usual interviews that resulted in the traditional "we will call you" statement, Rachel finally made an impression. On Tuesday, April 4, 1977, the first commercial job for Rachel in California was announced. It was for Heinz Ketchup. The little boy in the spot with her was "Sparky Marcus "(Issoglio). For those old enough to remember the cartoon, *Richie Rich*, Sparky was Richie's voice.

This job might not have been if it weren't for Sparky Marcus' mother, "Skeets" Issogllio. I had taken the car to work, and unknown to both Rebecca and me, MGA was going to issue a "wardrobe call" for Rachel. The agent called and informed Rebecca that Rachel was required to be on set for this wardrobe call. Left with three children and an important callback, Rebecca had to improvise. So the then pregnant Rebecca, with only one maternity dress (the rest of the clothes where still in Utah) had to find a way to get 10 miles from their location. Still new to the community, she didn't know anybody she felt comfortable to leave the children with. Being in the pit of frustration, Rebecca made a sign that read "Desperate! Need a ride."

With children and suitcase for the wardrobe change, the family stood on the corner in front of Frank's Steak House on Vineland Ave. The intent was to wait for the bus, but inwardly, Rebecca hoped that they could get a ride, thus getting to the studio sooner. She fully expected someone nice would come by and offer the family a ride, so they waited and waited.

Finaliy a bus did come and they boarded it. Unfortunately, the bus let them off about fifteen blocks away from the studio. It was getting dark and they were more than ninety unprofessional minutes late. Unknown to Rebecca, the studio had hired a back up, in case Rachel didn't show up. When the pregnant and exhausted Rebecca came in with three children and dragging a suitcase, she evoked a myriad of emotions by the on-lookers. As Rebecca gravitated to the circle of the other mothers with their children, all who seemed to be dressed in the latest fashions, one of the mothers inquired about the Jacobs' tardiness. The woman, Skeets Issoglio, Sparky Marcus' mom, made all the difference.

She forcefully told Rebecca, "The next time you have a problem, and you call the agent and tell them to make arrangements for a ride! Eventually, Skeets took Rebecca under her wing and told her some important "ins" and "outs" of the business. This was Rebecca's initiation into what is known as "The Moms' hotline."

About this time the casting director had zeroed in on Rebecca and rudely proclaimed, "Rachel was so late that they had lost any chance in keeping the part." Feeling stunned and helpless, Rebecca was paralyzed by the situation. Skeets then stepped in. She went up to the casting director and told him the story of Rebecca's effort to be there. Rebecca watched in awe as this "pro of surviving in Hollywood" did her work on the director, by whom she was not in the least intimidated.

Finally the director calmed down until he saw Rachel's hair curled. He then said, in no uncertain terms, “That hairstyle is not what I want.” Once again tempers flew and he protested saying that her hair was "terrible" and then yelled, "RE-CAST” while walking away. As hot tempers subsided, the make-up artist came over and took the curls and put her hair up in pigtails, which eventually became a type of trademark for Rachel's commercials for a few years thereafter. Rachel finally filmed the commercial and won respect of cast and crew and the client.

Rachel's remembrance of that commercial was a reality shock of how commercials are really made. One aspect that seemed odd to a six year-old girl was the fact that she was not allowed to eat the hot dogs she bit into for the commercial. They had a bucket nearby and after each bite, following the director's call of "cut." Rachel had to spit it out into the bucket. After dozens of takes, the bucket was full and Rachel had her first taste of how disgusting commercial making can be!

Rachel and "Sparky" performed the commercial as brother and sister. They would work again together in the fall. They not only became friends, but so did their parents. In fact, we thought so much of the nice family from South Pasadena that we sent in a missionary card to the California Anaheim Mission headquarters. With white shirts and ties, two clean-cut, full-time missionaries paid a visit to the family. Before very long, some good Lutherans became good Mormons.

Unbeknown to the Issoglio family in California, at the time of their conversion, their other children, in other parts of the country were also investigating the Church as well. Eventually, they all joined The Church about the same time. Part of the missionary tool used in Skeet's conversion was an experience of *Saturday's Warrior* as performed in the Pasadena Civic Auditorium. They came away from the performance definitely impressed.

The Heinz Ketchup commercial was an early confirmation that we had made the right choice in coming to Hollywood. At that time we had no idea of some of the risk factors involved in making commercials. Later we came to learn that a commercial may not air for months or sometimes never!

Also, the money that the actors earn by making the commercials was contingent upon the market in which they played, and when, or if it played. Some commercials may be filmed a year in advance, and actors may have to wait that long for a residual paycheck. We were in desperate straits at the time of this commercial. Immediate funds were sorely needed!

Fortunately, for us, the Heinz commercial aired in two weeks and the duration of the commercial was long. The family got checks every week following the first airdate, and this provided a steady supplemental income for the better part of a year.

The work with Doty-Dayton Motion Picture Production and Film Distribution Company was exciting for me, but short lived. In June, the Doty-Dayton company went out of business, an all too familiar pattern in Hollywood, particularly companies offering wholesome family entertainment. I remembered the advice of Lex de Azevedo, who said, "If you're big on the *show* but little in the *business,* you will ultimately fail." Doty-Dayton had over-extended its means and couldn't pay its debts. After the Sheriff came to lock the doors permanently, I was blessed once again through church association to receive employment.

I found an empathetic, spiritual giant of a man, looking for some help, and I went to work for Keith F. Barton's small construction company. The circumstance was uncanny. One of Keith's clients was Mr. Robert Sallin, director of Rachel's Heinz Ketchup commercial. He told me, "She is not only such a sweet girl, but she takes direction so very well!" He added, "The Heinz Company had budgeted a huge amount for the current advertising campaign, and Rachel's commercial was one of three which the third-ranking executive in the company said "was one of the best ever for them."

Before the children started to win opportunities for various parts in commercials and T.V. series, Rebecca and I had made the decision to hold some standards and values in the representation of the work that we were a part of. Being L.D.S. and from Utah, we obviously stuck out as being more than a little different. But trying to instill a solid base for our family to grow from, we sought to share our talents only in projects that were of worth and of good taste. This is an oddity, in contrast to the undercurrent forces of Hollywood, which play upon the desperation of actors, causing many to compromise their dignity and integrity in order to survive. For us, the choice of following Christian standards had been made before we left the state of Utah.

It might seem that this would be a weakness, but be it remembered that another Utah family proclaimed unapologetically that they were members of The Church of Jesus Christ of Latter-Day Saints too, and the Osmonds survived the spectrum of their publicity. Our values were not a publicity ploy. Our religious beliefs were not something we wore for twelve hours a day; they were what we were and what we wanted to become. Our moral values set the agenda, no matter the consequences. To this end we often, both individually and as a family, knelt in prayer about job offers.

When we set up the boundaries of our relationship with Mary Grady, we asked that we would not be sent out on interviews for products that promoted tea, coffee, alcohol, tobacco, or other harmful substances. Later we would be told that these restrictions made the family seem too conservative and temporarily shut a few doors of opportunity. Indeed, a recent survey reveals what we didn't understand about the decision makers of Hollywood. "In 1983 a public opinion survey of 104 of the most influential leaders of TV's creative community showed a full 45 percent who claimed no religious affiliation whatsoever and 93 percent who said they seldom or never attend religious services" (Medved, p 71).

Chapter Seven

The Flipper

After the Heinz commercial, things really started to pick up for this little actress of ours. Toward the end of July, Rachel had performed an unusual feat in light of the win-lose ratio of jobs per number of interviews. Instead of the usual ratio, Rachel was "batting" an almost unheard of, three wins out of four attempts.

What happened before one of these commercials is both indicative of our values as a family and representative of the gumption that propelled us to Hollywood. During July, Rachel received an audition for a T.V. series that seemed a "tremendous breakthrough", but the show had an objectionable title. It was a debate within our family that participating in such a production would compromise our standards.

Having high moral standards in the entertainment industry of the post 1950's may seem to be a contradiction of terms. Indeed, we were unaware of the cultural shift that was occurring in Hollywood. Without outward rhyme or reason, Hollywood seemed to crave inserting innuendos and other objectionable speech into film and TV. A survey of Hollywood films in 1991 illustrates what was starting as a pattern when we were in Hollywood in 1977. "A breakdown of releases according to MPAA ratings shows that the average R-rated movie contains twenty-four F-words, fourteen S-words, and five A A-words—providing its viewers with a major obscenity every two and half minutes." (Medved, p181)

But we timidly took each step into this new experience with the faith that we would be blessed. It was critical for us to let our agent know as soon as possible about the part. Finally we told Mary Grady, "We will forgo this opportunity, but thank you for the offer." We expected to hear Mary Grady say, "You'll never work in this town again." However, no audible message of this type was ever vocalized to us personally, but nevertheless something very similar to that expression was felt.

Over the weekend, especially with religious services on Sunday, we had time to reflect and evaluate and appreciate. If virtue is its own reward, and it is, we made the right choice, knowing we would be blessed. In the next five days Rachel interviewed for four projects and won three out of the four ads. The spots were for *Der Wienerschnitzel, Mattel Toys*, and *Kellogg's Pop Tarts.*

Just before the filming of the Kellogg's Pop Tarts commercial, Rachel and Christian were riding in the car with their mother, returning from an interview, when a hard wooden toy was turned into a projectile, leaving Christian's hand and arriving squarely on Rachel's front tooth, thus removing the tooth. This was on a Friday. She was scheduled to film the very important Pop Tart spot early Monday morning. The food industry people are very, very particular about teeth when their spokespersons are pitching their products, particularly with cameras on close-up.

There were times in these interview situations where potential actors would line up in a row and smile as the casting director would go by and look and visually probe each mouth with scrutiny. It was reminiscent of ranchers at an auction, where potential buyers could look at the teeth of the horse to see if they wanted to buy. With teeth being so important, we were in "a pickle-of-a-bind."

We got on the phone and started calling for information. The best answer we felt we could find—and time was so incredibly tight that it did not appear realistically possible—was to get Rachel over to Burbank. There was a dentist who specialized in a plastic prosthesis. Later this prosthesis was given what came to be an almost endearing name for others and us in the industry as a “flipper!” This experience was all absolutely new for us, but we hoped Rachel would have her first "flipper" created to fit her mouth—if there were enough time to get there that evening, and if the dentist were able to accomplish it before Monday. Tough job. Was it answers to prayers? Probably. But it all fell into place with barely a minute or an ounce of gasoline to spare on either side.

Once the "flipper" was in hand, or in this case, in mouth, only half the problem was solved. How will Rachel be able to talk plainly, unaffected, and deliver her lines without drawing attention to the problem and away from the product? Fearing that the product's executives would detect a lisp, Rachel practiced over the weekend. The job required skill, talent, and the ability to go beyond that of just acting. If anyone could do it, Rachel could. And she did!

Rachel talked to a toaster she called "Milton." It seems reasonable that if one paid very close attention to her enunciation, one might just be able to detect something, even without actually identifying it: "Aha! A flipper!" More likely one would just think, possibly as the ad people for the project and the company representative for Kellogg apparently thought, that it was just the way a little girl talks, sort of, almost with a lisp. She pulled it off.

While we as parents looked on behind the shadows of the set lights, Rachel's most memorable aspect of the experience was the flip side of what happened in the Heinz Ketchup commercial. In this commercial she had to eat "Pop Tarts.".. all day long! To this day, she still has an aversion to Pop Tarts.

***

Because of the advice of a truly good man, Keith F. Barton, I hung up another tool—this time my hammer—to take down the yardstick and point to places on the map to make the Carden-Lee geography class more meaningful to my independent forth and fifth grade students.

I had worked as an independent contractor for Keith Barton from April through the summer, but as fall approached the Southern California area, I was offered an opportunity to be a teacher at the Carden-Lee Primary School where Rachel and Christian and later Parker would attend.

I asked Keith's advice about what might be the best thing to do. Keith, in his typical style of subdued but poignant wisdom, simply reminded me, "Is there any greater calling or work than that of a teacher?" Was that rhetorical enough?

After the mandatory certification classes, I was almost ready to get right into that classroom with the children, chalk in hand. But first, there was a type of ritual that Mrs. McDowell performed: questions and answers . . . and statements.

“Mr. Jacobs, it would be well for you to be aware that here at Carden-Lee, we search out only the best to be our teachers. As we have collected our core teaching group, we have discovered something quite amazing, and that is that each of us, in some way or another, has a common tie with the name “Lee”. That is why it is `Carden-*Lee*.' Do you have any connection with that name?"

My reply. "Mrs. McDowell, would it be of interest to you to know that `Lee' is my middle name?" The job was in the bag.

About a twenty-minute drive from the heart of the San Fernando Valley, north, there lives and almost breathes a very popular amusement park called *Six Flags Magic Mountain.* The parent company budgeted funds for a regional television commercial. Rachel interviewed to be the actress to help advertise the fun park over local and regional television stations. She got the job . . . sort of!

Actually, unbeknown at first to her or her parents, the part had temporarily gone to a little boy, but the next morning, the boy didn't come through and Rachel was slipped into the spot.

At Magic Mountain, if you are just another customer at the park and are under a certain height, you are normally not allowed to go on some of the rides, such as the Colossus, a gigantic roller coaster. But if you are a seven-year old little spokesperson actress for the park for the day, even if you are way, way short of the minimum height requirement, that's different . . . you may ride all you want! Actually there was serious work to do. Acting is work, as actors especially know and as people who work with actors know. But Rachel was "required to ride" the big roller coaster and to perform a few other daring and exciting feats above and beyond the duty of her normal actress work.

Can you imagine my surprise (it was no surprise to her mother; she was there that day with Rachel) when the commercial came on television, and there was Rachel with her arm around a huge, living, breathing, almost salivating African lion?

Although Rachel had appeared on several other commercials up to this time, they were normally shown in different market areas, outside of California. The Magic Mountain commercial was shown locally. To actually see a person you know on television breaks a dimension and the flavor of television viewing is forever changed as you see dual representation of the same person. It's shocking, sobering, and simply breathtaking, simply wonderful!

The commercial ran so much that it would not be an exaggeration to say that it fairly "saturated the market." For months, three hours after school you could see Rachel's commercial 9 to 12 times a day. Some time after the discontinuance of the Magic Mountain commercial, I read in a local trade publication, (such as *Hollywood Reporter* or *Variety*) that the Six Flags Magic Mountain Corporation had increased its revenues and profits tremendously during the past quarter or two. My immediate response was, "And I know why!"

Around this time, we went out for family night at *Shakey's Pizza* in Beverly Hills, near La Cienega and Hollywood Boulevard. It was the first time we had ever been to that place. We were still feeling rather new to the community. While we awaited our simple order, we enjoyed the over-fifty-ish, gray-haired gentleman dressed in a red and white striped vest, shiny shoes, and matching striped vaudevillian type hat, playing piano.

He was really pounding out that Jazz and popular Ragtime, tunes. He motioned for the family to come over to his piano and sing along with him. It was a familiar song and the place wasn't very crowded. We sort of looked around and thought, "Why not?" During that first song, the piano player, Gordon, had been listening to our family more than we had realized. He then asked Rachel, "Do you know `California, Here I Come'?"

Rachel and her friend Rachel McDowell, and I had sung it almost the entire length of the return trip from Utah after the latest *Mailbox* filming, including a few additional, original verses we had made up. Did she know it? She had no sooner started to shake her head up and down in a "Yes" answer than here it came on the piano.

Her solo, with gusto!

Bravo! Much applause!

As the pizza order was arriving and the rest of the family began returning to our table, Mr. Driggs pulled me aside and said, "There are not two people in eight hundred with a voice like your daughter's. I have been in entertainment all my life; I'm not kidding you. Listen, I am in charge of the entertainment for the opening of a big shopping center in San Diego in two weeks. Could your daughter be one of the participants?"

“Well . . . I suppose so", I said.

Telephone numbers were obtained, and even though Mr. Driggs had told us it was "a contest," the full impact of that concept did not really sink in until we were at the mall that Saturday morning, surrounded by what seemed like thousands of hyper-tenacious shopping mall lovers.

“There's the stage, Rachel . . . there’s your accompanist . . . good luck . . .”

And perform she did! Her performance was about in the middle of the show, being before and after both adult and teenage and other youngsters' numbers. It felt like the talent show scene in Salzburg in *The Sound of Music.*

“And the winner is . . . Miss Rachel Jacobs of North Hollywood!"

That was fun! Especially to have it over with.

During the month of April we were able to move from the upstairs two-bedroom apartment into a little green, two-bedroom house on Vineland Avenue near Burbank Street in North Hollywood. Our less-than-ten-blocks, away move kept many things the same, regarding both school and church.

After a few more commercials our direction seemed more defined. As acting became the focus and close-up of our lives, like a camera iris, all the peripheral and background became extraneous and lost relevance as a realistic means of serious pursuit. However, many experiences were less glamorous than what might be imagined by those that consume T.V. rather than produce it. By attending what is termed in the business, "cattle calls" or interviews, where there are so many people present, vying and competing that one's identity is nearly on the level of cows during transport or auction . . . or slaughter, as the case may be and sometimes is—Rachel emerged with a triple line-up of *The Paul Lynde Christmas Special*, *The Mac Davis Special*, and *The Robert Young's, Father Knows Best Christmas Reunion.*

In between the explosion of parts for Rachel, some of the same people who had produced the *Saturday's Warrior* that we had been involved with in Utah, were going to cast in the Southern California area to do a touring engagement with the same show. Performances were to be in cities up and down the Pacific Coast, with other performances in Phoenix and Las Vegas. Rachel was contacted to see if she would be interested and/or available to take the part of "Emily" again. The commitment was made. Her mother would again be part of the chorus, and there was a new wrinkle: before the tour was over, our new baby, Tyler, would make his stage debut, but with a *pink* ribbon attached to his beautiful little bald head.

The Paul Lynde Christmas Special came as a result of being informed of the project and then of the audition time and date by one of Rachel's wonderful teachers at Carden-Lee, Miss Virginia Lewis, a former actress herself as well as a concert violinist. Virginia's friend, Jenna McMahon, was a writer/producer on the show, and when Virginia told Jenna about Rachel, Jenna thought there could likely be a part there for her.

Since the Mary Grady agency had not contacted us about the audition, Virginia Lewis suggested that they circumvent the agency and go to the audition.

The audition went as they typically do: get a bunch of kids together, then select two of three kids that they want, but don't let everyone else know.

When they got to the studio for the audition, Rebecca said that she was with the Mary Grady Agency. Later, after we actually got the job, the studio called the agency to tell them about their casting of Rachel. Rachel was so new at the agency that initially the sub-agents in the office that day didn't even know who Rachel Jacobs was. When they figured it out, Dick Woody from the Agency called up very upset, perhaps partly because the family was out doing what an agency was supposed to do.

It is obvious that they didn't know Rachel or didn't think she could handle the job if she wasn't told about the interview by the agency. The pecking order would dictate that Rachel needed to work her way up the ladder and pay her dues. Rebecca played dumb, but in the final analysis it appeared that the agency wasn't looking out for Rachel nor did they ever know her potential. Although that was a breach in policy and procedure, it was not "illegal, immoral, or fattening." Watching out for your children, and knowing their potential is a parent's stewardship, right, and responsibility.

Even though we landed the job independent of the agency, essentially doing the job of the agent we had "signed on" with, we were willing to honor the contract to pay the ten percent from the production company, even though they had not been responsible for getting Rachel the job. Instead of an apology from the agency, and a sign of recompense from them by sending Rachel out on many more interviews, the sub-agent under Mary Grady came across very angrily as if he had personally been upstaged and circumvented.

Nevertheless, it was a delight to actually work with some people Rebecca and I had grown up watching on television and others we had watched a bit after we had grown up. People, like Martha Rae, Lonesome George Goebel, Foster Brooks, Ann Meare, Paul Lynde, Anson Williams, and others! Rachel was to have—the whole family was to have—a very important experience regarding the work on this show.

Rachel admired Paul Lynde. She had seen him on T.V., and like a child, she was honest and accepting. But, Paul Lynde lived so close to the character (sour grapes) he personified, that he didn't quite know how to take Rachel who was so forthright and sincere. He was a comedian who needed to upstage to be funny. And Rachel was a child, who by nature, upstages anyone, but not maliciously.

This combination had all the ingredients for war. During the blocking session, where every actor is told where to go, on what line or cue, Rachel firmly fixed her position for one particular part in her mind. As they were rehearsing the scene, she was corrected by none other than Mr. Lynde.

Lynde blasted her with. "You're not right!"

Rachel was all too honest and spoke back to the star and said kindly. “No, you’re not right."

Then he said, “You don't know what you're talking about!"

The script supervisor then stepped in to let each go to their respective corner. She then checked the script. In the green room, where parents went to watch their children on camera fed from the studio, a silent tension filled the room as this dialogue unfolded. Rebecca waited for the script person to end this confrontation. With three ringed binder in hand, the script supervisor scurried through her notes. Rachel was correct! They would do the scene as originally blocked, as Rachel had remembered it. Big tension: a seven-year-old telling the boss he could not possibly be right!

But being upstaged, even if legitimately, can from a poisonous retribution. Everyone assumed that the conflict was over, dead, buried, and decomposed. It wasn’t, at least not for some factions. On taping day, when Rachel had the ending line, which was really cute and spot-lighted her, the begrudged "big shot" actor threw in a comment of his own, which wasn't cute, clever, or funny, but which accomplished at least two things. First, it was a deflation of Rachel's line and made her unfairly lose prominence in the scene, and secondly, this act drew unworthy attention to Lynde. This was an unwelcome, albeit valuable, experience which taught the family about the nature of ego in the industry. Fortunately, even though it was the first such experience, it soured the milk a little. One nice thing that Rachel remembers are the kudos that came with the Paul Lynde Special, such as a large arrangement of flowers and her own dressing room with a fancy lettered plate name attached on the door and a candy basket. Rachel felt like the real star that she really was.

On Wednesday, October 9, 1977 (Paul Lynde Christmas Special) Rebecca sustained a ferocious headache while on set at KTTV Channel 11, Metro-Media Square. Some of the valiant helpers of the day were Skeets Issogilo and Vini Francis and, of course, Dr. La Clair. We would be seeing more of him in about two weeks when Rebecca's baby was, in Parker's vernacular, "really done."

I replaced Rebecca on set. Rebecca was to be "bed-bound for two days" and "drink lots of liquid," especially cranberry juice, and take Vitamin B^6 and Niacinimide," as per Dr. La Clair's advice. Because of the demanding schedule of filming that Rachel had accumulated by the fall of 1977, our family had come to an unexpected realization about our future. Living in Utah and just thinking about being successful in the industry was easy compared to the actual work of all members of the family. To be successful, all hands had to come on deck and pitch in, offering what talents they could. It was a continual effort to get out there and be at auditions on time wearing the right thing, and saying the right thing, and leaving at the right time.

The maxim: "nothing ventured nothing gained" certainly applied to this situation. The normal family that sits down every night and reflects about their day was not so for our family. We did most of our reflecting in the car driving after school, arriving on the set early to begin filming, interviewing, and learning together. Someone had to brush the hair and choose the wardrobe, provide the transportation and the breakfast, lunch, and supper; and the entire intellectual, social, emotional, and spiritual nourishment that fed these little actors in between jobs and even on set.

At that time both Rebecca and I had acquired headshots and composites and had worked up our resumes. I was active in attempting to promote our own careers as well as those of the children. Economic sense weighed twenty-five dollars a day being a school teacher against two hundred and fifty dollars a day on any standard union job.

Who better to be with the children than the child's own loving, caring, doting, and adoring parents? The reciprocal learning between child and parent with the heavy time factor of being together so much, especially meeting new situations together at the same time and coping with conditions as a team was a marvelous character-shaper and bond-builder.

As a family, in order of priority, after our commitment to and activity in the church, there was the BUSINESS. For it was family business. Our family was our business. Our business was our family. This isn't so uncommon in other family units such as in the community in Idaho, which we had enjoyed so much being a part of. Potato harvest was a family affair. Planting and farm chores, the full spectrum of that style of life demanded a team effort. We were experiencing the city version of the same work ethic of Southern Idaho.

While on the Paul Lynde set, I received a totally unsolicited compliment from the director of the show, who said, speaking of Rachel, "She's incredible! One in a hundred. . . just tell her what you want and she does it. She's a natural." Even though Rachel got most of her jobs because of her bubbly personality and exuberant talent, her style as a child actress was reduced to one major contributing factor, she was obedient. She would do anything that was proper and descent. There was a trust between Mother and child. And with that trust, Rebecca could direct Rachel in any situation.

For example, some time later, Rachel did a fast-food commercial and as they were setting up for the shot, all of the kids were squinting because of the hot reflecting light boards. Rebecca told Rachel to open her eyes. Even though it was so bright, she obeyed. While the other kids were still squinting, delaying the shooting of the commercial, the other mothers got clued into what Rachel was doing and started telling their kids to "do it like Rachel." Immediately after the shot was over, Rachel came up to Rebecca crying; she said that she couldn't see. Without permanent damage, she sacrificed herself. Rebecca realized then that what she should have done was to let Rachel squint and perhaps the crew would have gotten the clue that the lights were too bright.

***

Rachel was interviewing for a Century 21 Real Estate commercial, which was scheduled to cast on October 25, 1977, the same day when our baby was due. In case the baby came the day of Rachel's audition, an actress named Judy Haller, a friend of the family, would pick up Rachel and take her to the filming. Parker and Christian were also to be "farmed out" upon notification.

On the 25th, at 4:30 a.m. Rebecca awoke with strong contractions. At 6 a.m. she woke me. In preparing for the new baby, Rebecca and I had made a thorough study of options and had decided to "go natural." We called the midwife; by 6:30 she was there. She put Rebecca into the bathtub with extra warm water. The buoyancy factor of the water relieved much of the "bearing down" sensations and discomfort for a short time. By 7 Rebecca was back in bed; the assistant doctor, Dr. La Claire, had just arrived, and by 7:30 Dr. and Mrs. Eddinghausen were there.

By this time Parker had been taken to some neighbors, Rachel was in her bedroom getting ready for her commercial, Christian was at the foot of the bed ready to see his very first birth, and by 8:30 Tyler Grant Jacobs was officially a member of the family.

Dr. Eddinghausen walked me through a little cutting-of-the-cord ceremony. Neighbors Diane Giles and her mother, Sybil Howard, came over and helped clean the baby and dress it, and applied foot and finger massage (reflexology) to Rebecca. Judy had come by and picked up Rachel, and Diane's husband had picked up Christian for school.

It was a wonderful experience!

Later that day, on set somewhere, the Century 21 people were still deciding who, out of the several highly qualified little actors and actresses they had assembled, would be their choice for their principal lead or spokesperson. So they asked a question that fell in favor of Rachel's answering it better than anyone else.

“Did anything exciting happen to anybody here this morning?"

“Yes!” said Rachel.

“What?" they asked.

“I had a brand new baby brother, right at home!"

They picked Rachel. Who could top that!

And she did them a good job and made some good friends with the other children who filmed with her.

From this commercial, Rachel would become very recognizable wherever she went. This high-powered campaign saturated the market; but this time, not just on the local or regional level. This was national. People would even ask for her autograph. In the business this was called a "high T.V.Q." It got to the point that when our family went out, people would come and ask if she was the Century 21 girl.

Century 21 liked her performance so well that they cast her two more times in later spots. When the commercials aired nationally, they featured Rachel at their national convention in Las Vegas, where she shook hands with the company president and signed a lot of autographs. They even gave her their little five thousand dollar dollhouse that looked like the real one she was standing beside in the commercial.

When the offer of Century 21 was initially talked about with the agent, we were told that the whole package would probably be worth twenty thousand dollars. The actual paycheck was about two thousand dollars. This disparity was brought to our attention by Grandpa Alden Richards, a program manager at KSL-TV in Salt Lake City. He bought the commercials for the station and had assumed that due to the amount of airtime, Rachel was making a lot of money.

What often happened in "the biz" was the producers would pick unknown talent so that the price for acting would be less. Also, the check from the client went through the agent. Most agents that enjoyed any sort of longevity had developed a good sense of the delicate balance between the casting agents and the production and ad people. They were careful not to out-price themselves, while at the same time giving the impression to their bread and butter, the actors, as being considerate and devoted. They offered the worn out phrase, - "we're looking out for your best interest."

In the most cases, getting jobs ended up being a biding contest between the agent and the studio, which wanted to get quality talent for the cheap price. Strange bedfellows are often made behind the scenes. Regardless, we humbly accepted their pay and were grateful for the opportunity.

Despite what Century 21 Real Estate agents may have believed, despite what family members and relatives might have thought, despite being asked to film a second and third commercial for the company at not a penny more than the first one (which is absolutely outrageous), and despite being promised by the agent that there would be some "real good money" coming, it never, ever happened!

Chapter Eight

Try Again

The first week of December 1977 we returned once again to Utah so that Rachel could film another movie of Uncle David's titled *Uncle Ben.* It was a true story as told by Dr. Kenneth Mcfarland about a town drunk whose sister died, leaving three small children. The story was about change and forgiveness, as Uncle Ben tried to convince the judge to grant him custody of his two nephews and niece (Rachel). Uncle Ben was played by Dr. Keith Engar of the University of Utah Drama Department. It was a successful short film that was circulated throughout Utah and the L.D.S. church worldwide.

Then back to North Hollywood. It was December 20; a year had passed since our family had made the trek to California. It was a good time for reflection. Even though our immediate answers to prayers about the move had not been answered, we now had a strong feeling of confirmation. We made more income in that year than we had made in the last three years in Utah. Certainly we felt good about the previous year. Our children had come out of relative obscurity, without a circle of high-powered friends or influential people to help them break into the "biz." Indeed, *Saturday's Warrior, The Mail Box* and *Uncle Ben* were important credits, but they were never considered major factors for winning future opportunities. Casting people were looking for the right fit, despite Rachel's Utah credits.

From our viewpoint, the next year looked extremely promising. I wrote in our journal: "Today we are preparing for Christmas. We have made some little baskets of almonds to give to friends. Our family once destitute, living in a high maintenance apartment, had been given a Christmas by anonymous strangers. Now in service, we attempted to give others kindness for the love that was shown us. Financially we can't believe the income! Now we need to learn to control it better." For a season, things would be very prosperous, but this prosperity was a temporary thing. Show biz is a feast or a famine, with many hills and valleys of success and failure.

It might seem ironic that as a family we gambled on the acting profession but put values and faith above work, as so many can attest who have gone to

Hollywood and have been in desperation for "a part, any part". We felt and still feel that the reason we were in Hollywood was because that is where Heavenly Father wanted us. This central belief saved us and our children from allowing the illusion of Hollywood to capture our self-esteem or self-worth. Ego, pride, and perhaps a little arrogance all crept in from time to time, but mostly these feelings came from without. While within, a central thread bonded our family together to principles of the gospel, combined with a spiritual feeling of divine worth that goes far beyond discarded reels of edited film.

Often we turned down legitimate jobs if they interfered with Church affiliation or gospel principles. Such was the case when Rachel auditioned for a national *Orbit Gum* commercial. She was offered that part. The next day, January 6, 1978, Rachel auditioned for a *Homefront* commercial, and won the part. *Homefront* is a title for a body of commercials made for the Church of Jesus Christ of Latter-Day Saints by the Bonneville Corporation. However, the commercials had conflicting dates and she couldn't do both. This was a difficult decision; the national commercial meant better money over the long run by way of "residuals." The other, the Mormon commercial, was a "buy-out", a flat fee equivalent to two days' work. It became a family matter and a choice with some trepidation and not without consequences.

Feeling that the Church commercial would touch more lives and do more for the good of people than the all-important gum taste issue, we put our faith in Him who wanted us here and had provided for us. By living to a principal of promoting Christian values, we obeyed and hoped to be blessed. We chose The Church commercial. In this instance we were blessed both spiritually and temporally. The next week after the filming of *Homefront.* commercial, Rachel got three national commercials.

The set location for one of these commercials was in Cheviot Hills, just about three-fourths of a mile south of Twentieth Century Fox in southwest Beverly Hills, at the home of an artist and her husband. The well groomed, tastefully decorated home came complete for film with a white picket fence. The lady of the house, Elaine Livesey, the artist, asked if on another day or evening Rachel might come back to her house and model some old dresses for one of the artist's new paintings. It was agreed upon and at the end of the session, Rachel left with the original painting by Miss Livesey.

After they finished filming, the director and camera operator, Ron Dexter, pulled me aside and said, "Listen, that child of yours . . . has got it! She is rare.

You don't find one like her in four out of five hundred. I don't know what background she has, but she's great!" That is always nice for a father to hear.

Amid television commercials and one-shot specials and print work for Rachel, there were still a few areas of the business that were yet tapped into. One of these was a television series.

This opportunity came on March 31, 1978, just the day before the family went to Oakland, California, for a performance of *Saturday's Warrior*. Rachel had auditioned for a T.V. series pilot with the working titles of *Thirteen Queen's Street, The Better Half,* or *Five Marvelous Women,* and had been informed of a callback, which unusual as it was, was on Saturday and conflicted with the *Saturday's Warrior* engagement in Oakland that weekend. Every option was examined. People such as Rachel's friend, Rebecca Clinger, who knew the part, were asked if they would mind going to Oakland to play the part of Emily; but nothing worked out, and nothing seemed to allow Rachel to be at both events. The agent, Mary Grady, was especially insistent that Rachel would be giving up "the chance of a lifetime to be in a series" and to miss that appointment "would be a terrible mistake." A decision had to be made soon. Again, money could have been a deciding factor, but it wasn't.

As Rachel and I sat on the concrete stairs at Metro Media Square, I said, "Well, Rachel, What do you want to do?"

Rachel replied, "That's a big decision for a seven-year-old, Dad."

"You're right, Rachel, it is. But I know you will make the right choice," I replied.

Rachel thought and thought, as the two of us sat there, both of us were silently praying for direction.

Rachel broke the silence by saying, "Dad, I know what to do."

"What's that Honey?"

And in one simple statement, Rachel revealed the thought and intents of a pure heart.

"We could help more people if we did *Saturday's Warrior*," she said.

That decision proved to be the right one, even though we had been coached and coaxed into believing that if we were not there at the callback the next day, that that opportunity would be lost and gone forever. The family stayed in Oakland and over the weekend, the producers of the T.V. show allowed Rachel to meet with them the following Monday. She got the part and shot the pilot. However, like eighty percent of TV pilots, this never went past one episode.

***

Ann Everett to the rescue once again! (They played mister and misses Santa Claus our first Christmas in North Hollywood) She knew we were looking for a larger place on a less busy street and she told us of a house for rent near her, 6213 Morella, North Hollywood. Universal Studios had acquired a number of houses and adjoining building lots along this street back in the era of silent films. This home, now owned by a Dr. Maitland and Annie Dirks of Lancaster, California, was just one of those properties. As the community grew, other houses were built on some of the adjoining properties, but the lot adjoining this house remained vacant, and thus there was a large house with a large yard instead of another house right next door.

The original residents of the house were the film actor John Gilbert and his wife, Latrice Joy, contract actors with Universal Studios.

Other desirable features of this new place included the storage space, a built-on garage with doors, an inside laundry room, a huge family playroom, an automatic lawn sprinkler system, a bimonthly maintenance crew for the yard, a playhouse, leaded windows, a living room with a wood-pegged and grooved hardwood floor, a vaulted ceiling, good colors, and a concealed room behind the hinged bookcase.

In May of 1978, Dean Moser, who hired me at the ill-fated Doty-Dayton company, asked if I would like to come on board as casting director assistant with sundry other duties which included screening scripts. His main assignment was to cast for the movie *Rivals* or *Stranger at Jefferson High* an NBC television special. There were many former television and motion picture "stars" who basically all went through the same process of being notified by their agents about the interview, receiving "sides" in some cases, and finding the production company location, signing in on the "sign-in" sheet at my desk, then given additional "sides" or part of the script, and then waiting their turn to be seen.

I learned about the other aspect of the "biz" of Hollywood while working on this production crew. There are enemies from without and from within. I would use my own vehicle much of the time when errands were to be run. The production manager's job was to hold down costs and to bring the show under budget. The letter of the law was observed when it came to the lawgiver, in this case, the middle-aged, extremely high-salaried, with a huge bonus at the end of the show, "slickster". Other people who ran errands for the company received reimbursement by the mile, including the production manager, but when I requested reimbursement, it was tallied a different measurement, that of estimated miles per gallon.

There wasn't much difference, but the per mile standard gave me, provider of five dependents at minimum wage earnings, little advantage. I mentioned this impropriety to the producer/director, who in turn mentioned it to the production manager, who in turn intentionally left my name out of the credits of the movie.

Illusions in the back of the camera were sometimes as real as the illusions in front of the camera, as we were beginning to realize. In the advertising business, what you see in the picture, either still or on video, isn't necessarily what you get. Christian's picture appeared in several local newspapers and catalogs wearing clothing that was literally pinned in the back, so that it was form-fitted just for him. We wondered about the ethics of this situation since perhaps hundreds of thousands of customers purchased these clothes, and then wondered why they didn't fit their son like the picture showed.

Rebecca received a call on one occasion from a former neighbor friend who said they "absolutely loved seeing Rachel's bedroom set" on a recent commercial for a product Rachel was "pitching." Her reply was becoming familiar:

"Well, that wasn't really Rachel's bedroom set. That was a film set in a studio where Rachel was advertising this product. And that very shiny floor you mentioned... that wasn't ours here at home, there were about three people who worked on that set floor and they even lowered the actor onto it with a crane so as not to put scuff marks on it..."

Toward the end of the summer, both Rachel and Christian were cast as brother and sister in a project called "*Visions*". Even though this was a nice event of some measured success, Christian was becoming a bit discouraged with all the many interviews he was going out on without getting very many jobs.

As is true with perhaps most siblings, Christian had a different personality and style separate from Rachel's. Christian was and is an extremely innovative person. Even when he was a child he didn't come to an audition and sit with obedience in the same way Rachel did. As a child he wanted to do things his way. So he would do it his way and if the director liked it then "great" and if the director didn't like it, then he was not cast. In the beginning of his career, he struggled like many learning the mystery of what the casting director wanted. Christian did very well in his initial interviews, but that's where it seemed to end. After numerous second interviews or callbacks, Christian was given the nickname in the Jacobs household, as the "Call-Back Kid".

However in February of 1978 he had a breakthrough and won a *Tommy Toys* commercial. When Christian and Rebecca went to an all too familiar call-back, the casting director noticed Christian's unusually attractive hands and asked Rebecca, if her five year-old son could play *Twinkle Twinkle Little Star* on the piano. Without hesitation she answered, "Sure!" Rebecca then took Christian to the nearest piano, and taught him the tune. The next day he taped his first commercial.

The one predictable thing about the entertainment business is that it is unpredictable. Soon a year passed with Christian going out on at least fifty interviews, but to no avail. Christian would always be one of the five out of two hundred boys chosen to come back for several interviews. But still, he would never get the job. At this point, he become very discouraged, and this endless cycle of not being the right height or having the right look was getting to the point of not being very fun. "Why didn't I get the part?" became a question that Christian would ask parents who were unable to give a satisfactory and convincing answer.

Finally, frustrated and worn out with the interviewing game, Christian announced that he would not go on any more interviews. Then an interview opportunity with EUE-Screen Gems, at Burbank Studios came. Christian definitely did not want to go and face another rejection. Giving in, we felt there were no longer any character-building factors about making him endure to the end. We made a deal with Christian, "Just one more interview. This is the last one. If you don't get this job, you can give it up forever."

The part called for a little boy who was supposed to fall off his bicycle and hurt himself. During the interview, Christian was directed to pretend to fall down on the floor and hurt himself. Being the innovative actor that he was, he jumped off a chair, impromptu, and faked an injury so realistically that the casting people really thought he had hurt himself.

Without a hint of expression, they thanked Christian, told him he could go home and they continued on with the other interviews, asking another boy—who had already been interviewed— to come back in after Christian had left. By interpreting what this tactic meant, it translated into casting death once again for Christian and we concluded that the other boy must have won the part.

Our whole family was disappointed and it looked like the end for the "call-back kid's" budding acting career. There were tears shed and hugs given. Then the telephone rang. It was the agent. Christian had just won the part of the little boy falling off the bicycle! He now had the weekend to learn how to ride a bicycle!

A truly great master of the media, Stu Haggeman, directed the commercial called *Try Again*. It went on to win national awards as a public service spot and was part of the Homefront Series, originating right out of Salt Lake City, Utah, and was an important public service campaign by The Church of Jesus Christ of Latter-Day Saints.

It seemed significant that on the very precipitous edge of a major "give-up" for Christian and our family, that he did "Try Again." We were grateful and valued highly the experience of working with the people that we did and for the experience we gained.

We felt that the production company thought that these being Mormon kids would make the commercial look authentic. Christian relates, "being able to be an influence on people just on the set and to be able to talk to people about the Church because we were Mormons was great." Many L.D.S. members don't realize that non-Mormon crews who probably didn't know very much about The Church, filmed these Mormon Church Commercials. We felt like it was a type of missionary work and a small but important service for The Church.

Early on in his acting career, according to me, but humbly denied by Christian, he reportedly became known to the production crews as "One-Take Jake," meaning that he could get the shot right the first time without having to do it over. Our children did what they do extremely well and casting agencies and product clients and advertising executives knew it.

By this time our family had somewhat settled into the irregular schedule of always going to interviews. In a sense, interviewing for acting jobs was just part of the chores. After school, Rebecca would get the children all cleaned up if there was time and then head out for interviews. There were sacrifices from the beginning of this chosen career. As children, their lives couldn't revolve around watching television or taking ballet or piano lessons or Scouting or baseball or a thousand other things. These exceptions are all a part the normal life-style of families who have children in "the biz."

There may have been a little jealousy among our children at times, perhaps due to the fact that each child was exposed to the art of acting at a young age and saw brother and sister being able to work on a fun project; nevertheless, it was a private victory of competition when the day arrived, on October 31, 1978, when Christian had three interviews on the same day and Rachel only had one.

Within this timeframe, Rachel worked on a phenomenally high-budget television series project masterminded by Fred Silverman. The series was *Supertrain*, a *Love Boat*-like show. Rachel was cast alongside Keith Mitchell as her brother. Keith was Jackie Coogan's grandson. Jackie's daughter, Keith's mother, was Leslie. Leslie and Rebecca hit it off the first day. More opportunities came along to work together such as on Gary Coleman's movie for T.V., *The Kid With the Broken Halo.*

During this time I had the opportunity of joining a special sub committee for Screen Actors' Guild. The purpose of the organization was to talk about the topic of minors in the entertainment industry. The timing for such discussions could not have been better as Rachel had just been hit in the head with a heavy bucket of paint in a stunt, miss-rigged on a "pick-up" shot for *Supertrain.* It hadn't killed her and it didn't put her into the hospital, but she experienced pain and soreness of some time. Even so, she was expected to perform in spite of existing discomfort.

Chapter Nine

They Got Away

In the beginning of 1979, something really big seemed to be about to explode upon the industry as well as the theater-going public of the United States of America. The famous comic-strip characters from *Annie* were to take on real people and this time, not just on stage, but on celluloid. As the call went out, agents were scrambling to notify potential talent. The Mary Grady Agency, now convinced of Rachel's ability, contacted us about the Annie part. Audition times were set. Musical pieces were rehearsed.

And the sun really did "come out tomorrow," but not for Rachel. After a year's preparation, she had survived two major cuts and the pick was down to a handful of actresses. As the main role went to another, Rachel was offered an understudy part of one of the orphans at the Shurbert Theater in Century City. Mary Grady suggested that Rachel would make more money if she stuck with commercials. We agreed.

One interesting footnote: In this yearlong struggle for Rachel and for the girl who actually won the part of *Annie* in the movie—despite a life-time of preparation in singing and dancing lessons for her and what her family sacrificed to have that happen—in the final analysis, the dog, "Sandy" came away with an equivalent, if not a greater amount of money, than did the actress who played *Orphan Annie*. Although exposure may have more worth than money initially, the tendency to underpay the talent, the human talent that is, is an inequity that still persists in Hollywood.

In March of 1979, Rachel auditioned for a part in new series, a spin-off of *Soap*, with Robert Guillaume, called *Benson*. Rachel was up against Missy Gold as well as others. Missy won the part on this highly popular and long-lasting series. Later going up against the Gold children for parts would not be an isolated experience. It is interesting to speculate how different Rachel's life would have been if she had won this part. Once again, the crest of stardom was in reach. Rachel was on the threshold of success, but it was not meant to be, apparently, for the time being.

The last part of March, Rachel had several interviews, one for a remake of the old *Mod Squad* television series. She had won that part and was to film on the next Monday. On the Friday before that, she was filming a *Hush Puppies* commercial in the La Canada/Glendale area. After a smashing Easter egg hunt, the next morning red spots began appearing on her face. By evening it had been confirmed; she had a full-blown case of chicken pox. She had to give up the *Mod Squad II* spot; and then every ten days to two weeks another of Rachel's' brothers came down with exactly the same thing.

At this time Tyler was scheduled for an interview with Reid Miles and Company. Tyler wasn't feeling particularly well, yet he had not developed red dots, but the rather frequent need to change his diaper. He acted lethargic and almost motionless. The casting people entered the room and scanned for the most quite baby. They saw Tyler and made their way through the other crawling and crying babies.

One of the casting people named Susan, drew close to Tyler and said, "I just love quiet babies." They swept him aside, asked some questions, called the agency, and Tyler ended up doing an admirable job the next day, even to the extent of throwing a kiss to the camera!

Chapter Ten

Different Strokes

In August of 1979, I took my three boys to Utah for a Jacobs Family Reunion. Rebecca and Rachel remained in Los Angeles for Rachel's filming of *Diff'rent Strokes.* In that episode, which has later re-run many times over many years, Arnold (Gary Coleman) with appendicitis, meets a cute little girl, Alice (Rachel) in the hospital. They share the same hospital room. Alice's father, played by Dabney Coleman is unable to change his bigoted attitude.

The experience of acting on *Diff'rent Strokes* brought to light many things about the entertainment business, of which we were still very naive. "The conspiracy" began when producers conducted a casting call for the part. After an initial interview they would have a small group of actresses come back for a second interview. They would go into a room for the casting call and get all the actresses in a line and the casting director would go up to a semi famous or well-worked actress and openly and blatantly praise and flaunt themselves over her. Then when they came to Rachel, they would pretend to barely recognize her even being there. They simply greeted Rachel by asking, "now what is your name?"

Why? They knew that they wanted Rachel from the beginning, but they played with her mind and manipulated her parents by making us think, "Oh, I'm so lucky to even be considered for this part, I'll be glad to take a dollar just for the experience." That was their agenda, to get good talent cheap.

After Rachel got the part, they read the script and all seemed well. When the two weeks of filming began, Dabney Coleman, a method actor, had manipulated the whole script and had added a scene in which the character Rachel played made a sexual innuendo to Arnold. The line went something like, "I think I'll go and change into something more comfortable." The comment was in bad taste and unacceptable, and most of all, this line was not in the original script.

Rebecca knew that if this line was put into the script, it would compromise our standards and the network would take this sound bite and play it as a teaser trailer commercial for the episode. So even though one might not see the episode and the context of the scene, they would hear that remark. During rehearsals, Rebecca vocalized her concerns to the producers and told Rachel not to say the line. As rehearsals continued, the director purposefully skipped that part of the script.

On Saturday night, which was the final taping (not in front of a live audience), the producers had cunningly and conveniently replaced the normal on-set teacher with a new, very handsome set teacher full of questions and conversation with Rebecca. During taping, the mothers were not allowed to be on set; they were placed with a T.V. monitor in the greenroom. As Rebecca waited, the new set teacher came by and started to talk with her. The T.V. in the room displayed a picture, but intriguingly had no sound. With Rebecca sitting there knitting, the set teacher started to really give Rebecca a pitch, and it became obvious that this guy had a hidden agenda.

His agenda was to distract Rebecca and to get her attention off the TV monitor. As the set teacher talked, Rebecca looked over his shoulder and saw Rachel mouthing the taboo lines over the silent screen. Rebecca stood up and said with determined exasperation, "Oh no you don't!" She left the greenroom and stormed into the sound studio, which was strictly forbidden during taping. Despite Rebecca not wanting to be the stereotype of a pushy stage mother, there was no one else to watch out for Rachel's best interests. Regardless of the stereotype and perceptions of others, Rebecca, with motherly instinctual intentions was there for protection—to be the bad guy if needed!

Before Rebecca went into the room, Rachel had been fighting her own battle of standards. One of the cardinal rules that Rebecca had set with the studios was that no mascara was to be put on Rachel's eyelashes. This had less to do with religion, and more to do with keeping a little girl a little girl. When Rebecca had left the staging area, the make-up artist came over and put mascara on Rachel's eyelashes. Rachel made up an excuse and she went to the bathroom to wipe it off. Later, when the scene began, she was directed with pressure to say the line that she didn't want to say. She was caught between professional adult authority and parental obedience. With no coaching and no protection from mom, Rachel was on her own.

Rebecca had arrived on the studio set like a cannon ball falling to its target. With a touch of a nervous quiver in her voice, but with determination, she announced,

"Ok you guys, you know that we were not going to do this!"

Then to soften this risky rhetoric of argumentation, she modified her intent and retreated her vocal force by saying, "Little grandmothers in Utah aren't going to like this." In hindsight, what Rebecca wanted to say is, "This is wrong. We made a deal; we are out of here." And then walk away. That kind of courage comes with experience and we were still very unsavvy about the rules of the jungle where we were by nature, the hunted, not the hunter; the prey, not the predator. So, inexperience and fear kept that scenario from happening.

When her objections left her lips, the studio exploded into a verbal barrage by the producer, director, and Dabney Coleman. They started yelling, exclaiming that Rebecca was a bigoted, self-righteous, snoot and was going to ruin the show. From their point of view, they thought the sexual innuendo was appropriate and Rebecca's objection must be centered on the fact that Rachel was white and Gary Coleman was an African American. The truth was, that Rachel was type cast for the role and it didn't matter to Rachel or her parents if there were little green boys or girls in the scene. What was of issue was the inappropriate allusion that the character Rachel was playing wanted some sexual favor from the character of Arnold.

As comments volleyed over Rachel's head, she became upset and ran to her dressing room. Rebecca, not making headway in the argument at hand, saw the direction of Rachel's retreat and decided to follow. When Rebecca came into the dressing room, Rachel's first words, pleading to her mother, were, "Where were you?"

This could have broken Rebecca's heart with guilt, but before she could answer, the powerful head producer came into the dressing room and said,

"I want to know why you won't do the scene."

As Rebecca tried to reply, he stopped her in mid sentence and said

"No! I want to hear it from her," pointing to Rachel.

After a moment, Rachel replied, "I don't know why I can't say it, I just know that it is wrong!"

"Out of the mouths of babes." This ended the argument and he left.

The producer relented. The line was out and Rachel was in. They finished the scene.

This experience punctuated the difference in values that we had, juxtaposed to those of Hollywood. Indeed, we came to understand that Hollywood is an island, isolated from the core of American values, self-consumed with its own voice and vice. We were lead to believe in this instance that we were not in touch with society. In essence, this experience and others proclaimed that traditional values were over in America. Yet a recent study shows a different picture, one that aligns with our values in the yearly 80's.

"87 percent of Americans never doubt the existence of God and 77 percent say prayer is an important part of my daily life"(Medved, p 256).

Chapter Eleven

Freeze-Out

After the *Diff'rent Strokes* episode Rachel had the opportunity to work with Gary Coleman again, on his premiere TV movie, "*Kid with a Broken Halo.*" This starred Robert Guillaume, who later starred on the series "*Benson.*" Also another primary actress was Lani O'Grady, Mary Grady's daughter and a principle cast member of *Eight is Enough,* where Lani played the brainy oldest daughter, Mary.

Rachel's performance was so outstanding on *Diff'rent Strokes* and *The Kid with a Broken Halo* that she gained the attention of some executives at NBC. They talked with the Mary Grady Agency about putting Rachel under a year's contract. Also the production company, Tandem, made a similar offer. The choice then was to either go with Tandem, an entity of NBC, or go under the larger umbrella of NBC itself. Each contract held an exclusive on Rachel for one year (or season).

One factor that was not calculated into the decision is the fact that Tandem was also the production company that produced *Diff'rent Strokes.* We were really uncertain what the best choice would be. Not knowing the benefits clearly and completely of either contract, we made a choice and the choice was Tandem. The exclusive contract was designed to keep Rachel available for Tandem Productions for one year. They paid Rachel $10,000 to just wait until they came up with a program or series in which she could participate or be the star of, like Gary Coleman's *Diff'rent Strokes.* Over the course of a season, promises of forth-coming work were made from the producers, but nothing ever materialized.

After the deadline of April came and went, the contract ended and Rachel was quickly and conveniently let go. Although the money was very welcome, Rachel was without exposure. Momentum and acting experience had been lost. We theorized that the studio saw that Rachel had talent and potential at that time in her career. But most importantly the studio saw her as a threat to Tandem's Emmy-winning series, the very popular *Diff'rent Stokes.* Therefore the studio wanted to keep her from going to on anther network, thus causing competition for their pet project.

This was a decade were many child stars were the centerpiece of a television series. This trend, although not new (e.g., *Leave it to Beaver*) had a cascading effect during the early eighties. Such shows as *Silver Spoons, Family Ties, Facts of Life* and *Growing Pains* were the big revenue winners.

It seemed that Tandem would be sensitive, given their success with *Diff'rent Strokes,* to child actors and their careers. But we didn't detect the hidden agenda until it was far too late. This, of course, is just a theory, but given the carnivorous nature of Hollywood, this scenario seems very probable.

While Rachel was on paid hiatus, Christian, Parker, and Tyler began to pick up work. Parker got his very first commercial for 7-Eleven. He was the lead. The other little children got to push him in the homemade go-cart along the sidewalk to their local Slurpee stop. It was "big-time" for him and for our entire family. In one year alone, Parker had accomplished a Herculean task for a six-year-old and had gone out on more than one hundred fifty interviews. He had landed fifteen local, regional, or national commercials, plus print work!

While the family was experiencing success and blessings, the tutorial love of God was about to permit a traumatic event. When Christian was so convincing in the *Try Again* audition, making them think he was really hurt, little did he realize that a year later, life would imitate art, as the motorcycle he and I were riding met a truck which pulled out suddenly in October of 1979.

Three weeks later, the day before Thanksgiving, six-year-old Christian and I were released from Cedar Sinai Hospital in Beverly Hills, almost walking on my own and Christian with his full spiker cast, sporting a stainless steel wheelchair. It was miraculous both were even alive!

In the beginning of 1980, Christian was gaining his own exposure. Some of the commercials that Christian did during this time were *Woodsy Owl, American Dairy,* and a memorable commercial of *McDonald's* with his brother Tyler and another up-coming actor, Will Weaton. Will would later go on to do many things such as the movie *Stand by Me* and as Mr. Wesley Crusher on *Star Trek: The Next Generation.* Christian and Will would continue to see each other at other interviews and callbacks. To this day, Christian still considers Will a good friend.

After Rachel's contract ended, she went back to the cattle calls and won a commercial in June 1980, for the product *Tang*. When we went to the initial interview for the commercial, we were told by the production company that they were looking for a dancer. Rachel had had *some* ballet, perhaps about six months worth. Upon arriving at the interview, there were many dancers present, complete with slippers, leotards, tights, leg warmers, and anything else that could be impressing and deflating for any other actress competing for the part without these accouterments. Despite a myriad of auditions and experience, Rachel and I nearly walked right back out the door when we saw the arsenal of competition. Instead, as inconspicuously as possible, we signed in and drifted into obscurity among the other hopeful actress.

When it was finally Rachel's turn, she left my side and like so many other times before, she faced the familiar anonymity of the interview situation. She had been behind the closed door for a minute or two when I heard spontaneous laughter through the door. As Rachel emerged, there was an air of confidence about her. Amid all those *dancers*, what the casting directors really wanted, was an *actress* . . . who could sort of look like she could dance. Rachel was perfect!

Rachel filmed the commercial with Florence Henderson of *The Brady Bunch.* Over a short period of time, Rachel was proving to be a profession while on stage. During rehearsal, the director wanted Rachel to swing her arm out a little wider as she did "The Tango," but Rachel suggested she would be "out of frame" if she did that. They rehearsed it, and sure enough, the cameraman said, "She's right." So they stuck with how Rachel had been doing it and it worked out very well.

A word about stars such as Florence Henderson: They are most often very wonderful people. Florence was an absolute angel! She was sweet and kind and went an extra mile to show her caring for Rachel. After the shoot was over at the end of the day, Rachel changed her clothes and took her costume back to the wardrobe department. As Rachel handed the clothing back the wardrobe director, she handed Rachel a package containing leotards, tights, and leg warmers. With this material, was attached a picture postcard of Florence and *The Brady Bunch,* with a sincere "God bless you, Rachel," signed "Florence H." During the taping of the commercial, Rachel and Florence were talking, and Rachel had mentioned that she admired the dancing ensemble that the other little girls in the commercial were wearing. Sensing Rachel's wish, Florence kindly and graciously granted it by later purchasing these items for Rachel.

In October of 1980, Rachel won a role on the popular series *Love Boat.* It was a two-week shoot for a double episode, which originally aired in October of 1980 and February of 1981. The episode featured the classical guitarist and comedienne-entertainer "Charo." Rachel played the daughter of Larry Linville, better known as Frank Burns on the series M*A*S*H*. This was a marvelous experience, as people were met, and some were worked with, who were truly legends. One of the stage's First Ladies, Lillian Gish, was there; Donald O'Connor's hand was warmly shaken; the singer Jack Jones, and of course, the *Love Boat* cast and others were there.

In November, Christian did an *Hour Magazine* guest appearance with Gary Collins in which Christian demonstrated a type of comedy kit. After this, Christian had his own experience with the dental appliance, "the flipper." Before leaving for the interview for an "Alpha-Bits" commercial, his mother told him, "Now, Christian, if you want this commercial, you will need to have your flipper fit you correctly. We can't get to the dentist before you go to the interview, so do what you can." She handed him the flipper. He snuggled it firmly into place, reshaping it by his manual insistence and perseverance. Finally, it felt and looked acceptable. Off he went, and he got the commercial!

December found both Parker and Christian performing the part of "Tiny Tim" in two separate productions. Christian was playing in *Christmas Carol* at North Hollywood's Theater Exchange, and Parker was in *Scrooge* in Studio City's L.D.S. Singles' Branch. Both Christian and Parker had solo singing parts in their respective plays and both did very well, not only in their parts but also in supporting the rest of the cast.

In August of 1981 Rachel auditioned for and went back to several callbacks for Dick Van Dyke's special, *How to Eat Like a Child.* The casting calls attracted hundreds of "the best," both in the area and from far away, who could carry a tune well and move their feet as though they were coordinated. Good little actor-singer-dancers (the "Triple Threat" in the business) were competing for parts. Rachel not only got a part, but hers was the little voice that said, "Project Peacock will be right back after these messages." Other children that were in the special went on to become very famous, such as Corey Feldman who was and is naturally funny.

This year Christian would do the voice of "Young Bambi" in voice-over work on Disney's 1981 remake of the audiotape of *Bambi.* Christian followed after Rachel and appeared on a *Love Boat* episode. Christian played the son of

Battle Star Glacticta's Richard Hatch. Lorn Green and Dorthy McGuire were also on this episode. The activity of Rachel, Christian, and soon Parker and Tyler in the advertising and show business world was nothing short of phenomenal! The words of Ruth Hale seemed to haunt and humble me during this explosion of success. According to Sister Hale, "people can live and die on the fringe of this business and *never do a commercial.*"

Later that year, Parker had won a part on ABC's new late night show called *Fridays*, which was a response to NBC's long established *Saturday Night Live*. Parker played opposite Rich Hall, who was playing the part of a reporter doing a story on apartments that did not allow children. This skit was a spoof on the extremes that children go to to get into these adults-only apartments. Parker was dressed up as an elderly gentleman. Parker recalls that he was in make-up for a few hours to get just the right appearance. His new persona included a bald cap, gray hair, and a mustache.

What happened right before taping was an example, once again, of putting standards before career and of the egocentric agenda of Hollywood. The director wanted Parker to pretend to smoke a cigar or at least have one in hand, which Parker didn't mind because he was a kid, and if they told him to do something, he would do it or endorse it. This situation didn't feel right to me. It could be argued that it's just an act, and Parker wasn't advocating smoking. But the principal on avoiding tobacco was a solid tenet of our faith. To participate in a skit that promoted this activity would call into question those standards. After all, shouldn't we avoid the very appearance of evil? It was time for principle to come before price or pay, so I gently pulled Parker aside right after the prop person handed him the cigar, before he was to go on stage. I looked down into my son's eyes and said, "Parker, this is not something we should do, even if it is a joke." With this Parker went on without the cigar.

Looking like an old man, with a white shirt and tie, a three-piece suit with a trench coat and a briefcase, he stood in deception while interviewed by Hall. Trying to foil the ploy and expose Parker, Rich Hall asked in a wise, sarcastic voice,

"If I were to give you this quarter, what would you do with it? Would you take it to the arcade?"

Parker replied, "Well, I'd invest it in T-Bills and money market certificates."

Hall then redirected his next question, and asked, "Do you think this is a lot of money?"

Parker then said, "Frankly, it's not a realistic figure."

The end of the scene came and I awaited the director to blast me for changing the scene by removing the cigar prop. Remarkably, I didn't receive any fallout. Both father and son suffered no ill repercussions. Later in life, Parker was able to realize the awkward position that he was in and the ramifications of that choice. That candid conversation about standards was a teaching moment. It did perhaps much in shaping Parker's character.

Chapter Twelve

Sit-Coms

Although our children were successful in commercials and some TV specials, they had yet to enter into another dimension of entertainment, that of the weekly sit-com. Traditionally, before a weekly series becomes a reality, an experiment in audience response culminates into what the industry calls a "pilot." The purpose of a pilot is really to save the network money if the program is not a success. In June of 1981 a tremendous opportunity for Rachel appeared when she won the part on a new pilot called *Dear Teacher.* One of the other cast regulars was a promising young unknown actor namedTed Danson. Typically, this pilot had a life span of only one program.

However, in September Christian stepped forward and won a part on a new weekly series called *Maggie* starring James Hampton, Doris Roberts, and other fine actors. The show was based on Erma Bombeck's books and life. Due to her popularity, the series appeared to have great possibilities. The program *Maggie,* in comparison, was like a cleaner version of *Roseanne.* In the tradition of real life family humor, it was really a show before its time. Christian was able to spend time with Erma, who was simply a charming, adorable person to work with. Nevertheless, being before your time sometimes translates into poor ratings, and the network abruptly canceled the show.

When *Maggie* was officially canceled in 1982, it seemed like fate had taken away a great opportunity from Christian. Momentary defeat can be measured by one's perspective. Later, this defeat turned into a wonderful break for Christian. Because Christian was now free from any contractual obligations, he was able to obtain the part of "Joey Stivic" on Sally Struthers' wonderful, but short-lived, series *Gloria.* An interesting set of circumstances lead Christian to win the part.

The part of Joey Stivic originally belonged to another actor. But as rehearsals began, this young actor became a little terror and was very rude and difficult to work with. We were later told both by Sally and Carol O'Conner that the company thought it would be best to find another actor. To this end the young actor was fired and the producers began to look for another actor to replace him. When the Mary Grady Agency was called, Sally asked for a dependable child; Mary Grady wanted to send Christian. But before Sally ever saw Christian, Sally was insistent and wanted to know if Christian was a nice boy. When they met, the chemistry clicked and Christian was a nice boy who meshed into the cast perfectly!

Gloria was a spin-off from the long lasting, critically acclaimed, *All in the Family*. For Rebecca and me, being on set with such star power was magnificent. To see "the best" in "the biz" at work was a great experience. "The best" included people like Burgess Meredith, somewhat advanced in years, but always coming through in the end like the true Thespian trooper that he was. And Sally Struthers! Even though there were tense moments, she delivered the goods, time after time, take after take after take—you have to if you are to survive in that business. Not enough good could be said about her and her dedication to that show and her kindness and generosity and sense of humor.

The entire cast and crew were a joy and a delight to work with. They couldn't have been nicer to a little nine-year-old, Christian Jacobs, and his family! The cast was thoughtful enough to throw a surprise birthday party for Christian. This was a nice break from the routine. Sit-coms are work; lines must be learned and rewrites of the script come every day. By the time taping occurred, every actor knew every other actor's lines. But despite the work of the sit-com, it had its benefits, such as having, on set, a certified teacher spending one-on-one time with the children.

Working on a sitcom brings a reality to the old adage, "Hurry-up and wait." Because so many technologies must merge together, the actor can experience high stress waiting and standing around for his or her one moment to perform. For Christian and any other normal kid, it can be really boring, as you just wait around. A typical day on a sitcom starts early in the morning. The child actors have to go straight to the on-set school to get the 3-hours of school done. This is mandatory. In order to complete shooting schedules, the set teacher can offer the child the option of banking the hours so that when taping day arrives, the child actor is free for extensive periods of time. Banking occur when early in the week they will have the actor attend 5 hours of school, with only 3 required, two hours are then banked, or substituted from the total 15 per week.

While working on *Gloria*, Christian would come in on Monday, go to school, and then read the script with cast and crew. Then on Tuesday, rehearsals start. The cast would work the first two or three days in a rehearsal hall that has lines and blueprints of the set house taped on the floor to simulate couches and other furniture. This is necessary so that the actors and crew can move to the correct location during taping. By Thursday and Friday the actors and crew are on the actual set.

As the week progressed, a typical routine of the business would pull Christian out of school to block the first shot. This is where the crew puts Christian where he would stand and where they want him to move during a scene. However, most of the technical setting was done with stand-ins. These are usually hopeful enthusiasts that are on set and are put in the real actor's place. Then the crews set up the cameras, lights, and sounds stage and plan around these motionless bodies. In the meantime, Christian is ushered back to school to finish the adjusted school day. After the crew is ready, they then film the scene. The process then repeats.

Before taping day, the cast would do a run-through of the whole show. Every night the writers and directors would access the content and do revisions. Every day a new script would come out and the evolution from the original script could often dramatically change by the end of the week; even the plot or story line could totally change by the end of the week.

Thursday was block and tape day. The cast would rehearse everything with cameras, lighting and sound. And they would light everything up in the morning and the four cameras would get the different shots that the director wanted. The environment is really extensive and full of tense moments when that night they'll do a run through on camera for the producers and the writers, who assess the content and flow of the show. Then Friday, they come in about 1p.m.. and they tape, until 8 at night. At that time they bring in the audience and the cast would tape in front of them. However, this is not the finished product; they still have all the tape that they shot during the day on Friday, just in case the stuff they did in front of the audience isn't good enough. Often the program that the audience saw is not the same one they see next week on TV.

What many viewers don't realize is that most sitcoms are taped sometimes months in advance. For *Gloria*, the cast and crew taped several episodes before the beginning pilot aired nationally in September of 1982. This was an exciting evening for us as we sat in our living room riveted to the television. For Christian, watching himself on TV was not just an entertaining or passive experience, but an educational process where he constantly evaluated his own performance.

As the series progressed, cast and crew become more cohesive, more like a family. Like any family, they had their laughs, tears and practical jokes. Christian had developed a routine of friendly torment of the director. The director liked to smoke and Christian liked to sneak up behind the director with a spray bottle from the sets make-up and hair style person and then douse the burning nose of the cigarette until it resembled a soggy noodle. On one occasion, as the cigarette-patrolling Christian came in like a Ninja after his victim, he squirted the ashen end of the cigarette, but was caught in the act by the director. As the squirt bottle was confiscated, Christian ran away proclaiming victory by saying "Super Mormon." In good humor, the director retorted this proclamation as he threw the spray bottle in the trash saying, "Super Jew."

The life style while living on set most of the day was a wonderful membership into an exclusive club that few ever enter. For those close to the pulse of Hollywood, the illusions created on TV are rarely close to real life. One such example of this truth presented itself to Christian during his work on *Gloria*. During this time, the then tremendously popular Mr. "T" was working on an episode of *Silver Spoons*, which taped in the next sound stage over from the Gloria set. As he appeared outside of the Universal Studios sound stage, the child actors from around the set, who appeared on the other sit-coms, such as *Diff'rent Strokes*, *Facts of Life*, and *One Day at a Time*, swarmed around him. As everyone came up to meet him, Christian was standing off to the side, feeling that Mr. “T” was too busy with the other famous actors, so Christian didn't want to disturb him. As Mr. “T” finished talking with all the other kids, he noticed Christian and worked his way over to him. When he came over, looking down, over his gold chains at Christian, he said. "Hey, man. What's your name?"

Excited and nervous, Christian not knowing what to expect replied with a meek voice, "My name's Christian."

Mr. "T" then said without hesitation, "Oh Christian. I'm a Christian too. Why don't you come have lunch with me? Com'on, jog up to the commissary with me."

This was an offer that no young boy could refuse.

So the hulking Mr. "T" and the tiny ten year-old Christian ran up to the cafeteria and had lunch. During the course of the meal Mr. "T" said,

“Do you know what I like about you, Christian? Your name!"

Then the two talked about being Christian. Mr. "T" revealed that he was trying to be a good Christian and came from a good Christian family." Mr. "T" asked Christian how many people were in his family." Christian told him "five," to which Mr. "T" replied, "Wow that's a big family."

Then Christian, feeling comfortable, told Mr."T", "Yeah, my family's Mormon."

Mr. "T" said, "I don't know too much about Mormons. Are you from Utah?"

"Oh, my parents are."

Mr. "T" then revealed his agenda.

"You know one thing is definitely true about you, Christian, that is you're not afraid to be who you are. And that's why you caught my eye when I was in the other room, and that's why I wanted to have lunch with you. You're a good little Christian." Stunned by his remarks, Christian Jacobs from Ogden, Utah, sat there and smiled.

"Well, I'm going to go do some exercises and I'll see you back around the set later on today."

Christian saw him a several more times later on during the week. Perhaps Mr."T" doesn't remember Christian, but Christian definitely remembers the impression Mr."T" left on him. For Christian, Mr."T" was just a really "cool guy" and at the same time he was a really good Christian, with a good heart, and a person who believed in Christ. Perhaps Mr. "T" saw that element in Christian too. Through the transparent world of Hollywood, it was comforting to know that someone could see the pure heart of a young boy and be singled out over other kids the big stars—that were around the lot.

During the year on *Gloria,* Christian attended an on-set school called the "Embassy School" on the Universal Studios lot. In attendance were the child actors from *Diff'rent Strokes, Facts of Life, Silver Spoons,* and *One Day at a Time.* Even though Christian was in the ranks of the hottest TV shows in the country and among the privileged few, he felt like an outsider, separated from the mainstream, an objective observer looking in. This feeling was in part, self-induced; this was because he didn't fit in with the typical Hollywood crowd. The main reason was the fact that didn't indulge in their behavior.

The big thing in Hollywood, or Los Angeles for that matter and generally in America, is the tendencies for young people to try to cheat the law of the harvest and reap where they haven't sown, to circumvent experience with experimentation and try to act grown up. Youth have always tried to break the boundaries of their existence. The first of flight was to grow up, fast! Smoking, drinking, and immorality could give the false illusion and appearance of adulthood. In Hollywood and within the "Brat Pack," maturity was a commodity that could be bought with fame and money. For Christian, this world was as shallow as the illusion of being Joey Stivic. Founded and grounded in family and traditional values, Christian never really fit into that other world. To be a disciple of the "Brat Pack," one had to participate in an orgy of indulgence, which only gave the appearance of freedom. Initially, the invitations to become apart of "the crowd" were offered. They would invite him to parties and other spontaneous occasions of mischievous behavior. But when it became evident that Christian was unwilling to share the secrets of their sins and indiscretion, eventually, the invitations ceased.

There definitely was a little "Brat Pack"; at the time and the head of that pack was Ricky Schroeder. His motley crew, perhaps guilty by association if not participation, included many of the rest of the TV successful child stars at the time. The list would include in part, Jason Bateman, Justine Bateman, Todd Bridges, Gary Coleman, Melissa Melanoa, Corey Feldman and others whose names are unknown, like the Jacobs. The burnout rate was brutal even for the young. Some who sold dignity to run with the "pack" are hardly recognizable in a medium that they gave blood, sweat, and tears for.

The Brat Pack would all get together and go out to parties and dance clubs and do "some crazy stuff." Christian had a perspective on that life style. For him the business of Hollywood was fun, interesting, and great; but there was more to life than a life style of perpetual parities. Fame and power are enticing elements, and Christian or any of the Jacobs would readily admit that they were not above temptation. Nevertheless, in retrospect my children agree that perhaps fame was not allowed in their lives because Heavenly Father knew they could not handle it well. Fortunately, we learned through others' experiences and saw the snares of self-indulgences.

During this time, Rebecca was walking by one of the school trailers and overheard a pernicious dialogue between a young very famous actor and the set teacher. The teacher was trying nicely and patiently to encourage civil behavior. He responded back by saying, "Shut up. I don't need you. If I don't want you for a teacher, I can fire you right now." Then and there Rebecca knew from first hand experience that a child with that kind of power could be a dangerous person.

As filming for *Gloria* ended at the beginning of 1983, Rachel was finishing up a movie for TV called, *Who Will Love My Children?* starring Ann-Margret and Frederick Forest. It was based on a true story of a mother who, after being informed of her rapidly spreading terminal case of cancer, looked for appropriate homes for each of her children.

This movie made both for the big silver screen and for television was a real tearjerker; but more than that, professionally, it won the director, John Erman, an Emmy Award! Rachel was playing the sister to Tracy Gold, a talented dramatic actress, who later went on to act in *Growing Pains.*

One could feel the soberness with which Ann Margret approached her part. It was as though she were living the character she was portraying, both before the camera and off. Her role seemed never to end. There was an aura about her as she sat in her chair or walked to and from the wardrobe and make-up area that commanded respect. Voices that otherwise might have been a bit loud or even raucous were subdued in her presence. What control she commanded, not only of her own part, but for those about her!

From the outset of the show, Miss Margret distanced the mothers from her and from their children during rehearsal time. She didn't want to socialize with the mothers to the extent of stealing time away from bonding with the children. Her intent was to enhance her and their performance. During pre-production, all of the child actors and actresses worked with a trainer/therapist, in group activities that were designed to help all mesh into and blend with each other. This strategy and regimen really paid off when the camera began to roll. The feeling of unity, of "oneness" of the family, was felt both on and off the screen. At the end of filming, Ann Margret gave each child a Sweetish Pony doll.

One thing that Rachel remembers which was especially frustrating was the fact that she couldn't cry on cue during one of the scenes. Rachel was a tremendous comedic actress, while on the other hand, Tracy Gold, an accomplished dramatic actress, could cry on cue in a mere heart beat.

Within the year of 1983, all three of our older children, Rachel, Christian, and Parker, would each have their own television series to act in, on three different networks. Their agent, Mary Grady, would comment, "I've been in this business twenty years, both as a mom and as an agent, and I've never seen three members of the same family have three series, on three networks, all at the same time."

At this time Rachel was involved with a new show with the working title "It's Not Easy" for ABC. A number of episodes were taped for this pilot. Rachel played the granddaughter of Jane Meadows. Gerald McRaney was originally scheduled to be her father in the series, but he opted to go with another show, a hit that propelled his career, *Simon and Simon*. Christian was well into the production of Gloria for CBS. And Parker was working on *Scamps* for NBC. This pilot starred Bob Denver, the famous "Gilligan" of *Gilligan's Island*. The producers were Sherwood and Lloyd Schwartz. *Scamps* (with the working title of *3 to 6*) seemed to have the right stuff with the actors and producers to make a hit.

The Schwartz team, father and son, had been associated with a number of programs that had records of longevity and tremendous success. With TV series like the *Brady Bunch* and *Gilligan's Island*, the Schwartz's were hoping that *Scamps* would be no less profitable. Theirs was a powerful force during this period and the impression made on our six-year-old Parker was that the "Schwartz's owned television."

Initially, the producers didn't have a part for Parker, but when he was interviewed, he was so unusual and represented such an adorable, unforgettable character type that they wrote in a part especially for him! Among the cast was a familiar friend of the Jacobs children, Joey Lawrence. The children saw Joey at many of the same interviews, and Parker had worked with Joey once before on a commercial.

Although *Scamps* aired as a special, they were trying to make the show into a series. Parker, who was of a serious, yet easy-going temperament, remembers the most distinctive thing about "Gilligan" (Bob Denver) was that he was “old and looked different from the *Gilligan Island* shows.”

With a powerful producing force behind them, this special could have taken off and Parker's direction in life might have been drastically different than it was. Once again, success was measured on a different, perhaps eternal timetable.

***

In August, during this ride on the crest of success, we were invited to represent our agency at a Gala Event at the Coconut Grove Ambassador Auditorium on Wilshire Boulevard. As we made our way to the event in our nice but conservative Volvo, we noticed that we kept pace with a conspicuous gold Mercedes all the way to the hotel. When we arrived, the gold Mercedes followed us into the parking lot. We then discovered that the driver was Captain Kirk himself, William Shatner. This was just a sampler of the amount of star power that would be on hand at this event.

All the agencies sent their best and we were in the midst of stars such as Emma Sams, Joan Collins, Ray Bolger, and the list goes on. Excluding one-month-old Emily, the whole family came, with Tyler being the youngest in attendance. With the press hovering around the room and we feeling responsible to give a good impression for the Mary Grady agency, we became increasingly concerned with Tyler's table manners and behavior. Then it happened without warning, Tyler said, "Look Ma." As we focused on our son, to Rebecca's horror, Tyler had broken all etiquette by sticking two small green peas up his nose. And if that wasn't enough, he then tilted his head back, took a deep breath, closed his mouth, and blew them out of his nose. These two green projectiles few across the table into the middle of the room, luckily missing any celebrities. We all could have died with embarrassment. After a quick exit and lecture, Tyler, along with the evening, went on without further incident.

After Rachel's ABC pilot ended, she received fewer opportunities for interviews. Rachel was now attending public school. Her French class was planning a trip to France. In the tradition of typical parents we told her, "If you want to go to France, then you'll have to get a job. In a non-theatrical family, this would mean a part-time job at a gas station or waiting tables. But for Rachel, this meant a bit part on a sitcom or a commercial. And she did a small part on *Silver Spoons.*

The *Silver Spoons* experience was a different pace for Rachel. She was not in a lead acting role, but rather in a supporting capacity in the background.

Being on *Silver Spoons* would be a high profile job for any teenage girl, except for Rachel. While all the other girls flaunted over Ricky Schroder, Rachel was frankly not impressed and didn't have the desire to give him the time of day; which, if it where her strategy to get him interested in her, it would have been a great success. To Rachel's surprise her tactic had the reverse effect on Ricky Schroder. With every rebuff, Ricky got more interested in her. One occasion he called her up and asked her to go to a Prince concert. Rachel politely declined. As invitations and flirting persisted, the situation was somewhat irritating for Rachel.

Once, while on the phone with Rachel, Ricky claimed that he was eating Flintstones Vitamins and joked that he was going to O.D. on them. Rachel was not emotionally stirred and eventually ended up calling him a jerk. To this he declaimed back something rude and Rachel hung up on the most popular young TV star of the day. Without disappointment in Rachel's decision, Rebecca commented that almost every girl in America would have traded places with her for the opportunity to go out with Ricky Schroder. For Rachel, "big deal."

While working on the series, *Gloria* , we were a part of a coincidence that was very special for Sally Struthers. On one occasion we met the full-time Sister missionaries for The Church of Jesus Christ of Latter-Day Saints in our area. One of the missionaries was a Sister Flores. When Sister Flores discovered that Christian was working with Sally Struthers, she told us a powerful story. Several years previously, Sally Struthers was in a movie about Sister Flores' father, Ralph. In this true story, Ralph Flores, a pilot in Canada and Alaska, was giving passage to a young woman (played by, Sally Struthers) when the plane crashed. The TV movie, entitled *Hey, I'm Alive,* starred Ed Asner as Ralph Flores and Sally. The movie stressed the fact that Flores was a Christian and held strongly to his standards and religions convictions. During the ordeal, Ralph Flores maintained that as soon as his passenger would humble herself and read the Bible, they would be rescued, but not before. After 29 days of surviving harsh Arctic conditions, the pilot's stubborn passenger finally completed her reading assignment. They were rescued 15 hours later. It was an emotional and heart-felt meeting when we invited Sister Flores on the set of *Gloria* and meet Sally Struthers. Sister Flores thanked Sally for her acting role. For Sally it was a unique meeting and seemed like life had come full circle for Sister Flores.

We considered Sally Struthers a close friend. She invited us to parties and even went out to a movie with the family. She was in our home and we in hers.

It was this kind, sincere nature of Sally's that made it ever more painful when she called in the first of July in 1983.

When I answered the phone I heard a quivering voice, so typical of Sally Struthers. I could visualize the tears streaming down her checks, and a particular acting hallmark of hers was the quivering chin. Surely it was now quivering.

"Kim, they've canceled our show!"

"Oh no, Sally. Why?"

It's hard to know why some TV shows never make it. Sally said it was part political, "old promises to keep among top network executives." The nature of "the biz" had once again taken the current probability of success out of my family's reach. If *Gloria* had continued, Christian Jacobs may have become a household name.

The irony was that *Gloria*, according to the past 12 months of the Nielsen Rating, had reported that the show was right at the top of the national public viewers' preferences. The show was on an upward trend, gaining a 12 spot, a 10 and finally an 8 week after week, while shows such as *Silver Spoons* and others were way down on the list, not even seriously competing with the popularity that Gloria earned and enjoyed.

Within a year, all three children were on promising sitcoms and then suddenly the carpet of fame and fate was pulled from underneath them. It would seem that three children on three separate networks could achieve some sort of longevity. But, perhaps we were not meant for that kind of fame and fortune.

Chapter Thirteen

A Good Turn

Often the person closest to the business is the person who is the least listened to. Rachel was being sent out on a new pilot with a story line that centered on ice-skating. So Mary Grady sent Rachel down to train with a coach to learn how to ice skate. Rachel was an okay ice skater but not a masterful performer. As she practiced and practiced, both mother and daughter kept thinking that Rachel's friend, Heather Hobbs, deserved this pilot, mainly because she was such a proficient ice skater. Rebecca called the casting director and said that Heather Hobbs, represented by the Iris Burton Agency, should be on the call. The casting director said, "Well, Iris doesn't have her on this call, so she isn't on this call."

Rebecca couldn't get it out of her mind. It just felt right. The casting director wanted a dark-headed ice skater and that was Heather Hobbs. Finally, unable to put the issue at rest, Rebecca called up Iris Burton, who had the reputation of being a challenging person to work with at times. Rebecca said, "I think Heather should be on this call." Iris replied, "No"! However, seeing an opportunity to promote her agency, she then proceeded to schmooze Rebecca into changing agencies. When it became evident that Rebecca was not interested in changing agencies, Iris ended the conversation by saying:

"If you were an agent, would you send her out?"

“Yes I would," replied Rebecca.

Iris relented, "Okay, I'll do it."

When the casting agent weighed all the factors, he chose Heather Hobbs. Rachel took a figurative step backwards and let the right person get the job. Although the pilot never accumulated into a weekly series, for Heather the experience will always be remembered. For Rebecca’s effort, Iris sent her a bouquet of flowers.

After the explosion of acting accomplished by our children during 1983, we sat down and tried to do some strategic planning for them and us. One of the realities was inescapable: our children were growing up. As we looked around at different agencies, we realized that although Mary Grady had kept us busy for seven years, her expertise of influence was centered more on young children, not young adults. We wanted to hook up with an agent who could move in different circles.

Around this same time another event influenced our decision to start looking for another agency. A dear friend and neighbor, Ann Everett, asked Rebecca if she could help get her children into the business. We had just helped a little neighbor boy get into the business and he earned twenty thousands dollars his first year. So why not? Rebecca went to Mary Grady and asked if she would represent the Everett family; Mary said, "No." Then after Rebecca begged, Mary Grady reconsidered and she said "Yes." The Everett children started out doing some print work. Initially it was nice to see friends when they went to interviews. Todd Everett and Christian were of similar ages and likeness and the success of one helped the other. Eventually, while on the interviewing circuit, our families, regrettably it seemed, started to become competitive. As a result, we were losing our friendship. We didn't feel good about this situation.

Since we had other options for acting, this contributed to our choice to find another agent. Over our years in Hollywood we learned some keystones of truth about agencies. The key is to find the right agent for your needs. Some agents specialized in voice-overs or print work. The Mary Grady Agency specialized in children acting in commercials, movies, and TV shows. There are a lot of scams within agencies. If an agency asks for big money up front or fees for acting lessons, then they are not to be trusted.

Finally, we decided to be represented by the Harry Gold Agency. Harry and his family had worked hard and worked smart and were well respected in the Hollywood community. The move to the new agency, was great for Christian, Parker and Tyler. But with the Harry Golds' daughters, Tracy and Missy, the move was devastating for Rachel. This is the same Gold family that produced Missy on the TV series *Benson*, and Tracy Gold on *Growing Pains*. Harry Gold didn't have any boys in his family and few in his agency, so the Jacobs boys opened up a new market for Harry. In hindsight we should have found Rachel another agent.

After we had left the Mary Grady Agency, Dick Woody from the agency called wanting to know why we had left. He was told the full story and the feeling behind our move. With no surprise to us, Dick said, "Had we know that, we would not have not sent the Everetts out any more." "I know," Rebecca replied, "but that solution didn't seem fair to the Everett children."

Soon after we had switched to the Gold Agency, an event proved our suspicions about the process of natural selection in the wilderness of Hollywood. When *Growing Pains* was originally being cast, Rachel was going up against Tracy Gold for the part of Carol. Christian was going up against Kirk Cameron for the part of Mike. And Parker was going up against Jeremy Miller for the part of Ben. Christian was too young—Parker was too old. And finally it was down to Tracy and Rachel. When the last callback was issued, the agency sent Rachel on a wild goose chase. They sent her to a building in an obscure location, where no one had ever heard of the production company. After a momentary spat of confusion, Rachel immediately got to a pay phone and called the Gold Agency. Concerned that she was going to miss this critical producer's callback, she asked for the correct directions. They replied "Don't worry about it." Held captive by their withholding of information, Rachel had no choice but to go home and miss the interview. Tracy Gold got the job!

Obviously the family, and especially Rachel, was upset at these series of events. But anger, without direction, is a self-consuming toxin and Rachel eventually got over it. Some time later while Rachel and some friends were at a U2 concert, they ran into the Gold family. They were leaving early and happened to have backstage passes. The Golds' graciously gave the passes to Rachel and her friends. This seemed to patch up Rachel's wounded heart. The loss of the *Growing Pains* job is the big "what if" for Rachel.

As Christian shifted in age and redirected his acting career, Parker stepped forward and won a spot on *Charles in Charge* in 1984, which was a great opportunity for Parker. They wanted him to be a recurring role in the show. As the season ended, the announcement came that *Charles in Charge* was canceled. The *Charles in Charge* episode was indicative of so many other series opportunities that passed Parker by. It was fun working with Scott Baio and his vibrant personality.

Christian was busy with various projects; one worthy of mention was an episode of *Highway to Heaven.* Christian took note of Michael Landon. He was a really driven person who knew the direction he wanted to go. As a director he was in charge, in a proactive way. Landon was really nice and very dedicated. He knew where he was going and what he wanted to get done.

In 1984, a friend of Rachel's, Sidney Penny, was cast as the lead of *The New Giget*, a remake of the original teen beach movies. Sidney wanted Rachel to play the part of one of her friends on the series. The description of the character was to hang around the beach in a swimsuit. Despite issues of modesty, Rachel was shy, and didn't feel comfortable standing toe to toe with beach babes who were models with perfectly curved bodies. Rachel appreciated the offer but turned it down.

In 1985, Rachel won a part on *Family Ties*. The particular two-part episode centered around the issue of book banning. Rachel was in both episodes. What was unique about this situation is Rachel's feelings about Michael J. Fox. After working around some of the biggest teen idols in the business, finally Rachel had a crush.

Rachel, who had performed in front of thousands of people, was stricken with a severe case of shyness around Michael J. Fox. Fox was truly a celebrity of magnitude even then, and Rachel felt genuine intimidation. One day, during rehearsals, Rachel was in the background wearing a shirt with big bold letters reading " THIS IS A DRUG FREE BODY!" Michael Fox came over to speak with Rachel and was looking for an ice breaker. Being observant, he saw the T-shirt and asked Rachel, "Not even Aspirin?" Rachel, for the first time, was star struck by this impromptu meeting. Unable to see the context of his question, Rachel stumbled and stammered and said, "AAHH, no!" Paralyzed in awe, Rachel was unable to carry on the conversation any further. Michael then walked away, probably thinking that she was a weird girl.

During the two weeks of work, one evening after taping a scene on the set kitchen in which Michael J. Fox was drinking a Pepsi, Rachel saw an irresistible temptation. Walking by the set, she found herself all alone, just her and the Pepsi can—the can that had touched Michael J. Fox's lips. It was the perfect crime: no witnesses, opportunity, and the motive of infatuation. So Rachel committed grand theft of a Pepsi can.

She kept this stolen memento for some time, but then trying to redeem herself, she donated the can along with a script of *Family Ties* to a celebrity auction.

Chapter Fourteen

Do Your Best

The move to Hollywood was a bit of a culture shock from the beginning for our family. We were exposed to a reality that some never get a glimpse of. We found there are good people wherever you go. Prejudiced of the unknown can be detrimental. Such was the case when Rachel came face to face with some non-Mormons. From her beginning career with *Saturday's Warrior* in Salt Lake City, she was not exposed to people who did not live the L.D.S. lifestyle. When we moved to Hollywood, such a consensus in beliefs would not be observed. When Rachel won a part in her first national commercial for Heinz Ketchup, she told her mother that she "wasn't going to do the commercial because they (the production crew) were scary because they smoked." This was a teaching moment for mother and daughter. Tolerance for others' creeds, faith, or the lack thereof, was an important issue for us to reconcile, first for ourselves as parents, and then to help our children.

When Rachel made her objection about the commercial, Rebecca explained the religious implications of "love for others," but for the moment, she told Rachel, "You forget about that and do your best." Such experiences taught all of the children to be tolerant and understanding of other's standards.

It didn't take our children long to realize that for the most part, their standards were at odds with the general population around them. If our lifestyle choices could have been kept in the context of everyday life, the adjustment may have been smothered. However, juxtaposed to our values, was an alternate demanding lifestyle of entertainment. On one hand, those within the industry had little understanding of L.D.S. values, which caused conflicts in otherwise compatible venues. On the other hand, those outside of the industry who associated with us could hardly understand the contrast and requirements involved in the entertainment industry.

Although I can look back at the years in Hollywood with more than a favorable view, the strain on the family or any family can be measured in the memory of what didn't happen or what the family could have achieved. As Rebecca would philosophically comment:

"Some say you can have it all!"

You can't! You have to make choices. Because Rachel would be filming a national commercial, invariably she would miss her bothers' or sister's birthdays. Because of work, Rachel didn't get to go to her prom. There are always choices that had to be made.

But Hollywood required a devotion to a timeline set by executives who could go home at night. To be a success, you have to keep going. The magic formula is up to what the producers are looking for. The producer may have an idea of a black-haired girl, so if a blonde comes in, then she has little chance. Rachel got the first job because she looked like the little boy playing her brother. Later in Parker's career while working on the Disney movie for TV, *A Fighting Choice* starring Beau Bridges, Karen Valetine, and Patrick Dempsy, one of the directors at Disney said to Parker, "It's a good thing that you looked like Beau Bridges or you wouldn't have gotten the job." So talent in some sense becomes irrelevant. There is not a magic formula except just being there at the right time and being persistent.

My children didn't always attend school functions, but we did the best we could. Their lives were full of new and exciting adventures; however, we didn't have the routine that most families do. In some respects, my children didn't learn to deal with boredom and consistency of doing just one thing. They faced some unique problems that other families didn't have to face. For example, on more than one occasion we were confronted with a dilemma of having a teacher being jealous of Rachel's or the other children's success.

This resentment stemmed from the fact that Rachel or any of the other children may do a week's worth of work and earn more money that her teacher would earn all month. If the tables were turned, in Utah, the oddity of a child star would have had the reverse effect. In some sense, in Utah they would have been respected. Yet in Hollywood, where teachers and school children see a plethora of child actors and actress, they gravitate to the lowest common denominator. They would see us as different, and project an air of indifference and intolerance of their status. The experience in Hollywood was a response that was often cool and resentful to their temporary fame.

These problems could not have been anticipated before we left for California. One thing that anchored our faith in participating in the entertainment industry was the example of the Osmond family and others we met along the way. Their success was deep in our minds when searching for a resemblance of comfort before we made the journey to Hollywood.

We soon discovered that it is possible to be good Latter-Day Saints and still be in the world, but not of it. From the beginning of Rebecca's and my courtship at BYU, we both aspired to work in the entertainment industry. Others would say, "You can't be in such a wicked industry and still keep your standards." What we discovered was that all people are made out of the same material. We were not super human, our children had talent, they had faith, and they were obedient.

As parents, we encouraged our children to not limit themselves. If they wanted to work on Wall Street or in the entertainment industry, they could do so, with honor and integrity. Why we actively pursed a career in a community that was amoral was a matter of determination. Why we placed ourselves within reach of some of the greatest temptations in the world for spiritual destruction, is perhaps answered by Christian:

> "I think we were so naive, that's probably why the Lord picked our family to do the things that we did, because we were so innocent. My parents were so naive about the whole thing, it wasn't like "wow, there's Robert Redford and all these great movie stars!" It was kind of like going to Disneyland and having a good time. After it's done, you just go home and go to bed. There was no hype or no glamour. I think that was the thing for us; we got to see both sides. We got to see people...which stars were nice and which ones were rotten to work with."

For all the descriptions of our life in Hollywood, many may have opinions about maintaining the faith while living so close to a secular non-Christian world. But in the analysis of our own lives, I'm filled with gratitude for the opportunity we had and the fact that we learned valuable lessons about life and about ourselves. Rebecca and I have accumulated a wealth of knowledge about the potential of youth of this world. We truly believed that age is not a measure of ability. In sum total, our life could be summed up in a reflective statement that is representative of many. As Rachel so poignantly states, "We're blessed."

Post Script: My Family's Epilogue

Rachel

One important event that pulled Rachel out of her self-imposed retirement due to the lack of jobs was an opportunity to attend a familiar casting call to be an extra on *Growing Pains.* Reluctantly, Rachel went to the all-too-familiar arena of the casting meat market. While at the interview, the casting people needed someone to say a line. Rachel volunteered, and they liked it. She won the part. Being completely unaware of Rachel's background, not knowing if she was in a union or not, they seemed too relieved when she affirmed her identity and her agent.

After the initial episode, they liked Rachel and brought her back for four more episodes, all a without contract. This meant that the studio wanted good talent without paying a lot for it. Rachel played the part of one of two air- heads who were friends of Carol (Tracy Gold). The same Tracy Gold who participated in the movie *Who Will Love My Children.* The initial plan for just four episodes ended up being seven episodes, still without a contract.

Growing Pains was a good experience and made Rachel feel successful again. It was reminiscent of what might have been if Rachel had won the original part. Meeting the cast was interesting. Having had the unpleasant experience with Ricky Schroder, Rachel was not going to go out of her way to meet Kirk Cameron. She didn't want to bug him. Her strategy was simple, "If he says 'Hi' then fine, I'll have a conversation." Hopefully more skillfully than her conversion with Michael J. Fox. However, "until then, I'll just keep my distance."

The second day of rehearsals, Kirk came up and introduced himself to Rachel. "Hi, I'm Kirk Cameron," he said. A conversion then ensued. Kirk went out of his way to put Rachel at ease. A good impression can be felt about Kirk. swooned over this then unknown actor. This would not be the only time that His up-beat presence on and off screen is accurate.

While on *Growing Pains,* Rachel was on set when a new actor broke into the business. The young, attractive boy was Brad Pitt. Even then young girls Rachel had the opportunity to work with Brad.

One reality of growing up was the change in roles offered to Rachel. She was no longer the cute seven-year-old girl in *Diff'rent Strokes.* As an adolescent, she got calls for adolescent roles. As she got older they wanted to cast her in roles which were consistent with the industry's perception of normal teenagers. Rachel received casting calls for parts that portrayed runaways, drug users, derelicts, and even received an offer to play the part of a prostitute.

In 1986 Rachel was offered a part on the series, *Cagey and Lacy.* After agreements were made, Rachel received the first script. To her complete surprise, the script called for a teenager who was coming of age and was "sexually active." The first show called for Rachel to be caught in the act, as it were, and they would show her buttoning up her blouse. This was completely unacceptable.

The real problem was the fact that the initial sides of the script, which she read in the interviews, didn't allude to the nature of her character. Rachel had no idea that this role included such graphic illustrations. This discovery occurred only two days before shooting would begin. To an industry seemingly without a conscious and morals, the mere suggestion that any modern actress would have a problem with this role was probably inconceivable. From the production company's point of view, this dilemma was not a dilemma.

Rachel called the agency to tell them that she would not take the part. Once again, threats and accusation were meted out and Rachel heard the familiar line: "You'll never work in this town again." Rachel did work in the town again but not for *Cagey and Lacy.*

In 1988, feeling that her life was slightly stagnate, Rachel decided to make a change, to position her life so that she could fulfill some other dreams. Glamour and fame might have been an objective, but the direction of the wind of fame is a fickle thing. Some who walk away from the business had been only inches away from the crest of success. However, the unknown nature of "the biz" might also predict that many are standing on the edge of a great chasm, with success on the other side. To this end, Rachel decided to leave the industry and move back to Utah to attend Brigham Young University. Ironically, when she told her Hollywood friends that she was leaving to go to BYU, their remarks were all the same: "What a shame to give up and leave this wonderful lifestyle." Rachel knew that there was something more to life, something eternal.

After a summer semester, Rachel decided that she wanted to volunteer for a mission for her church. This would require an 18-month commitment. The L.D.S. Church, being a lay ministry, meant she would have to gather funds from savings and from family to maintain her existence.

As she tried to secure funds for her mission, she turned to what she knew best. Through some contacts she had made while working on *Growing Pains,* she learned of a casting for *Uncle Buck,* the TV series. This was a spinoff from the movie. As usual, the series didn't make it, but it provided a start for Rachel's mission. While on set she would muse about the next year and a half as a L.D.S. missionary. After much anticipation, a letter came from Church Headquarters with her assignment. Rachel was called to serve in the Chicago, Illinois Mission in 1991.

While on her mission she had to struggle with her Hollywood past. Her first area as a missionary was around the Great Lakes Naval Base. This region is inhabited by fresh, out-of-boot camp young soldiers. The present and the past merged together because the *Growing Pains* reruns where saturating afternoon television. As Rachel came knocking at the door, she was often recognized. Once this happened, all discussion of the Savior and our Father in Heaven was replaced with, "Why did you leave Hollywood?"

This was a challenge. Rachel didn't leave her family for a year and a half to talk about Hollywood. Many are converted to the pull of fame, but few are converted to the gospel of discipline and obedience of God's commandments. This dilemma had an internal effect also. Rachel was struggling with her role and identity of who she was. For a year she questioned herself, "Am I a missionary or an actress?"

This was further complicated when Rachel saw a magazine with a picture of Brad Pitt. She later read the article and discovered that a turning point in Pitt's career was a role in the series *Thirty Something.* Rachel was up for the part as his girlfriend. This was after the *Cagey and Lacy* fiasco. However, due to the sexual nature of the script, Rachel had turned it down. Now reading the article, Rachel saw the possibility of how her career might have taken off. The thought of what might have been was self-consuming and Rachel wept as she put the magazine down. It was then that she understood the Lord's admonition to take up the cross and follow him. Without any further regret, her served the people of Illinois.

One eternal experience that her mission proved was the meeting of her future husband, Jonathan Struhs. He was originally called to serve a mission in Ecquador, South America. After arriving there and working for almost a year, the hills and terrain were affecting his knees, which were damaged from an earlier injury while skiing. To avert any other problems, they sent him to the states to get surgery. Then he was reassigned to the Chicago Mission.

Rachel completed her mission and returned home in April 1993. Jonathan was home in June and they got engaged in August. They married on November 24, 1994. After they were married, Jonathan told Rachel a remarkable story. Early in 1981, on one evening while watching *Love Boat*, Jonathan engaged in a ritual dialogue that involved his mother suggesting that any attractive young girl would be his future wife. As they both watched the *Love Boat* episode, his mother saw a cute little girl on the screen. She said, "Well you could marry her!" This exchange had happened many times before and after, but this time, Jonathan had a sliver of unknown perception and thought. He blurted out, "Yeah, I could do that." Years later he married the little actress who was on *Love Boat*.

Rachel's performing arts are presently limited to the 24-hour duties and obligations of a wife and mother. Rachel is not really concerned about reinventing her career as an actress. In retrospect, Rachel could have been Tracy Gold on *Growing Pains*. But if that had happened, she couldn't have gone on a mission. She might not have met her husband. So, the line of fate is forever altered. And what is to remain is unknown.

Christian

Christian was in Rachel's shadow of success from the beginning. This was sometimes frustrating, not because of the desire to be in front of the camera, but internally he wanted to do and be where Rachel was. When you're looking at the entertainment business from a child's perspective, you don't look at your career and say, "Well, here comes another stepping stone to my career...here comes another pay check to pay the rent." Instead, Christian looked at Rachel doing a *Der Weinerschnitzel* commercial and she was eating hot dogs all day. This is where Christian became jealous of her getting to eat hot dogs all day, or when she would do a cereal commercial and eat cereal all day. For Christian, it was all about having fun like Rachel. So the desire for Christian's acting career happened because he "would look at it from the standpoint that Rachel was having more fun than me!"

Soon Christian would gain a perspective on how much fun commercials can be or not be. In his own words:

> "I remember doing one commercial for *Handy Wipes*, it was a California produced commercial marketed in England. In the spot I had to eat a candy bar. The commercial took all day. With each take they kept breaking out new candy bars. At first, I was thinking, 'Yeah, this is great!' But, by the end of the day it was terrible. All the candy bars were making me sick.
>
> It's not as glamorous as I thought it would be, but even the term glamour for a child was not understandable. Commercials are hard work. The first commercial that I ever did was for *Tommy Toys*. I was on the set and it came time for my big close-up and I didn't want to do it, I was tired and I wanted to go home. I had been sitting around all day while they were setting it up. When the director came to get me ready for the shot, I said, Well, I don't really feel like doing it. I wasn't really afraid to say that then. Later I was told that you're not supposed to say that because this is your big chance. I've always felt comfortable being around the set and being around the people on the set. I never felt awkward or strange. I think it was like we were meant to be there."

Being in the entertainment business is hard, and even harder when your peers don't understand you. On occasion the children at school would make fun of Christian, mainly because kids will make fun of anything. For young children, anything that is not normal is a prime source of verbal attack. Not being able to be a normal kid was what it took to get a commercial or be on TV. You must go out and attend many, many auditions. Sometimes the family would go to six auditions after school, driving all over LA. Sometimes Christian and Rachel would have to leave early from school and get home at 7 or 8 at night. It was like an after school job. And at times, for a youngster, "It's a pain in the neck."

This lack of normalcy created a feeling of wanting to be like other kids. The irony is that you long for that which you can't have. As others envy the life style of the child actor, Christian would take the industry for granted, and spend his time watching all the kids around him and hope to be with them. The grass really seems greener on the other side of the fence. Even though Christian can now see that he was gaining more experience and knowledge than his peers in many ways, he was perceived as different. He would be on a movie set for a week and then come back to school, which was difficult for others to understand. It is hard to maintain friendships under these circumstances.

In retrospect Christian relates this feeling of being different in his own words:

> "I wanted to know what it was like to go through one baseball season without missing practice because I had to do a show or commercial. Sometimes kids would make fun of me and say things like, Oh, I saw you on TV" or "You're a nerd.
>
> Another reason that gave other children ammunition to fire at me occurred when I used big vocabulary words and a lot of kids thought I was nerd.
>
> My parents encouraged us to read a lot. This, along with acting where you're always reading, learning new lines and memorizing things, expanded my vocabulary. I think sometimes it was a bit odd to have a fifth grader saying big vocabulary words; so some kids would naturally make fun of someone different."

Even though having standards that were completely, totally different than everyone around you, talking to people about the gospel and other aspects about the L.D.S. Church didn't feel strange at all. During the year on *Gloria*, Christian was invited to a lot of network parties where there were all kinds of stars.

Everyone eventually, if not at first meeting, would find out that Christian was Mormon. However, their influence was felt more by the people behind the scenes more than by the stars and celebrities. This was because sometimes celebrities become "untouchable," even if they have a really nice personality, the nature of the business makes them almost inaccessible. A lot of the people behind the scenes, the directors, the casting people, the TV camera and lighting people were more influenced by the Jacobs' family than the actual celebrities themselves, perhaps.

Even though Sally Struthers was probably the closest we got to be with real star power, we talked with her just like normal people talk with one another. There were several times on *Gloria* when Christian started getting the fever of fame and feeling the power of recognition. In his own words:

> "I used to think, 'Hey, this is it. This is cool and where it's at' Yet at the same time, I always felt that there was something more...because show business is so shallow and changing. When I went on my mission, I found out what true happiness is. Happiness is being in the Gospel with a strong family."

In 1987 Christian worked with Christian Slater on Slater's premier movie called *Gleaming the Cube*. Christian can hardly be seen in the final version but during filming, Christian was on camera for much of the movie. During the few months of filming both Christian Jacobs and Christian Slater talked a lot and developed a close relationship. The strongest impression of Slater for Christian was that he was a person searching for something that he didn't know how to find. He was looking for a place to fit in. Even though now he has achieved a certain degree of fame, Christian would hope that he has found some inner peace.

Another friend from the business is Will Weaton, recently seen on *Star Trek: The Next Generation*. Christian and Will worked on a McDonalds commercial together in 1980. They have been friends ever since. They continued to see each other at many, many interviews. It's interesting to look at how their lives in show business have treated them. In some respects some might say that Will had a better life.

With an amount of wisdom, comes perspective. In Christian's words:

"Sometimes I look at people and see how great a person they could be whether they are a struggling unknown or a superstar actor or actress. Even people that weren't actors, I could see that sort of "searching sadness" and it didn't matter if they were the biggest star on the set or they were the janitor that swept up after they left. I saw a lot of emptiness or facades in the industry. One example of profound sadness was Corey Feldman. We grew up with him; he went to the same casting calls that we were at. Yet, we were in a different boat because we were members of the Church and we had different values and standards. But Corey Feldman, who was popular for a few years when he did movies like *License to Drive* and *Gooneys*, has had many personal problems."

Christian worked with Corey in 1990 on a movie called *Exiles*, produced by Disney. It was really interesting because Corey and Christian had grown up together. Christian saw so much sadness in him. He had such a good heart and was a good guy. Yet, he didn't have a solid religious foundation or the love that he needed. But he had the money to buy what he thought he wanted. Cars and other toys were his priorities. Corey was getting paid a lot for the movie and he made a lot of bad choices because he was searching for the quick fix to his problems. He knew that he had power on the *Exiles* set. Unfortunately a lot of the time he'd burn bridges by his attitude. You see this a lot in big stars like Madonna. They need everyone to look at them and know that they're in power.

Roseanne Barr was a lot like that too. Christian was on a *Roseanne* episode once. He acted in a little sketch. She was really bossy. She had a good heart but she would lash out at people and she even lashed out at the Mormon Church (not knowing that Christian was a Mormon). As she spoke this venom about what she didn't understand, I sat there thinking, "If you only knew. Here I was, a nobody, as far as the business goes, but I felt like I had it all. I could walk away from that set and the paycheck and it wouldn't matter one bit to me because it wasn't that important in the eternal perspective." For most of the famous, fame is everything to them. It is their identity, their whole world.

Christian could be found on many TV shows during the seventies and eighties, such as:

Cassie & Co (1982)

Strike Force (1983)

Posse

Visions

Not Necessarily the News,

Canterville Ghost

Henry Hamilton, Graduate Ghost

Second Sight (1984)

Pretty in Pink (1985)

Just the Ten of Us, The Tracey Ullman Show (1988)

"Kavin" on The Gummi Bears (1985)

Married with Children (1990)

Hard Times on Planet Earth (1990)

By 1990 Christian was eighteen and had a choice before him, an intersection that would alter his life. The choice was to either remain in Hollywood or do what he had wanted to do—serve a mission for the Church. This choice, like so many other choices for our family, was rippled with repercussions. At the time he needed to make the choice, he had completed a spot on the TV series *Major Dad.* The producers wanted Christian to have a recurring role on the sitcom. This would mean steady income and residuals when his episodes were rerun.

In some ways the choice was very easy. Christian loved acting, but he loved the Lord more. So Christian walked away from this opportunity and left for his mission in 1991. about the same year as Rachel's mission. Christian served his mission overseas, in Japan. Acting and his experiences throughout his life helped Christian gain a unique perspective about his role as a messenger for his Heavenly Father. In his own words:

> "What helped me on my mission was mentally putting myself in other people's shoes and presenting the message to other people the way I would want to hear the gospel if I were them. It's really important to know that you don't need to go much farther than your Book of Mormon or your room in humble prayer to know everything that you need to know or to have the Spirit. If I had become famous, I probably would not have discovered this fact. Going on my mission was not just for me, but for the people I was able to talk to and teach. If I weren't able to go on my mission or able to have that experience too, that would've been a negative thing. I think it would have been great if I had gotten this movie or if I would've been the one of the children in Poltergeist or *E.T.* But then again, money comes and goes and so money isn't all that important. When you need it, it is good, but the spiritual long-term aspects are more important.
>
> The Lord needs people out in the trenches...out telling other people what the simple truths in life are. Actors in Hollywood don't need to go to all the cast parties and be the glamorous people that everyone wants to be...It's just not there. There's as much sadness in a lot of those parties as there are in skid row places."

Even though Christian did numerous commercials and TV shows, today he has very little left over to show for it. Christian has a perfect perspective:

> "I think it's a blessing and at the same time I think it's a curse; but everything is how you look at it. For example, if you win the lottery, it is a blessing and a curse. It's a blessing because you can pay some bills, but it's a curse because, if you don't spend it wisely, then you've wasted it. Everything is a blessing and a curse."

One of these blessings or curses occurred at a crossroads in Christian's career in 1985, while he was interviewing for a role in *Mesquito Coast.* He was up against River Phoenix. Had Christian landed this role, it once again may have projected him in a new direction. Ironically, a few years before, River Phoenix's mother had asked Rebecca for some advice in getting her son into the "biz." Sadly to the loss of his family, and the public, a great light of potential was extinguished in1993.

Now Christian is pursuing music.

“I'm trying to get behind the scenes more and I'd like to eventually end up directing. Yet, I still love acting. I love to write and direct projects and star in my own projects, but not because I want to be a star necessarily. I would like to see a project all the way through. I'm kind a perfectionist and want the part to be right. If the director has a vision and the actors have the same vision as their director, it's easier to get a good product and be more of an influence for making something which reflect my standards.

The big dilemma for me is working in an unscrupulous, amoral medium. What’s a Mormon guy supposed to do in a rated "R" world? TV is still a little bit safe but at the same time, the way things are going, it's getting bad. As I act, I reflect upon my personal values, which are very different from the character. But at the same time, if I'm playing this character that is a total jerk, a murderer, or someone crazy, it’s just acting. Where do I draw the line?”

Parker

Parker Jacobs undoubtedly had his own impact in Hollywood while both Rachel and Christian were on their missions. Parker, with Tyler and Emma Lee, was following suite. Once the pallet tastes the insipidness of the experience behind the camera, illusion is lost forever. Parker realized this at a young age while acting in a lot of commercials. One such commercial was for *Kentucky Fried Chicken.* Parker spent the whole day, over 100 takes, saying, "This chicken's great!" Parker would then bite into the drumstick, hold, and then the director would say, "cut." Out of the camera's view, Parker would only bite a small potion then spit the chicken into a cup. Certainly, not a glamorous experience. If an actor doesn't eat the food that they present on commercials, then it is most definitely inedible, being composed of glues and other deceptive devices to make it better than reality.

During the years of commercials, Parker was chosen to work with then unknown Joey Lawrence in a hot dog commercial. At one point during the commercial with Lawrence, the director was tired of Joey doing a particular line and wanted a different voice. So he told Parker to learn the lines over lunch break and come back and tape that segment. This task illustrated the differences in some children when it came to acting. If Rachel had been given this task, she would have skipped lunch and become engrossed over the challenge at hand. Christian would have learned the lines, then improvised a few new expressions and added a few new words. Parker, on the other hand, when questioned while he casually ate lunch why he wasn't practicing the lines, replied, "I'm getting paid the same whether I do the voice-over or not."

In 1984 when Parker won a spot on the *Scamps* pilot, Parker's motivation was rather docile. It then became the responsibility of the resident actress in the family, Rachel, to motivate Parker. Rachel, then eleven, took this responsibility seriously, almost in a militant fashion. After pleading and persuasion, Rachel finally blocked Parker in a phone both, capturing him unconditionally. His only reprieve from capture was a considerable effort to learn his lines. The interrogation consisted of prompts and introspection into the character that Parker would play. She would prompt him by saying "Why are you saying this? Who are you saying this to? Why?" followed by commands of "Do it again. Do it again ..." These drill sergeant techniques worked, and Parker performed superbly in the pilot and learned to motivate himself better. At least he wanted to avoid another telephone booth experience with Rachel.

In 1985, Parker did a commercial at Six Flags Magic Mountain amusement park. This exposure had a more riveting effect on Parker than it did for Rachel. While at the theme park for a promotional, the feeling was odd as a crowd literally chased him down for an autograph. Parker would later admit that it was "kind-of cool" being instantly popular. But soon the experience became annoying. By the end of the night he was telling people to "leave me alone, I'm not a big star."

In 1986, the educational process of this child actor was hardly over; in fact it would take on a new dimension. Parker won a spot as one of the children of the new and hopeful *Valerie Harper Show.* At least that was the way it was supposed to be. The original title of the show was *Valerie's Family.* While on set, rumors had circulated that Valerie had fallen into disfavor with the production company's administrators. Rebecca asked Valerie what was going on. Valerie replied, "Oh nothing, only rumors." However, behind closed doors, disputes between Valerie and management intensified. Finally, an impasse was reached, which ended with Valerie getting fired from the project. This was sad for Parker and Rebecca. They both thought Valerie was a great and gracious lady.

Parker and cast were half way through the initial block of pilot episodes, with the lead actress gone. Shooting the rest of the episodes was impossible. The cast went on hiatus for an undetermined time. While the cast was gone, the production company scrambled to find another lead actress. They hired Sandy Duncan and re-titled the show *The Hogan Family.* The shots with Valerie Harper were taken out and redone by placing Sandy in the scene. Filming resumed, but once again this series was short-lived, and Parker was on the move looking for work.

In 1987, CBS found a home once again for Parker. The series, *The Cavanaughs,* was a carryout for three years. It started out in mid season with abrupt breaks in filming as the studio experimented with the program's time slot. Time slots, which are crucial to the success of a new series, are like a roulette table in some respect. The executives couldn't find an adequate time slot. For three years they experimented to find the right audience and to increase ratings. At the time, the impression given out by the production company was that the show was a success. Only insiders knew the true fate of the program.

Parker played one of the grandsons along with Danny Crooksey, the enduring character Sam, from *Diff'rent Strokes.* Both Danny and Parker were good performers. It became frustrating and sad because neither of them really got to shine. This was due to the tension of a new show that wasn't a big success. Following a code of professional tribute, the producers focused on the main characters. The series *Family Ties* was in a similar predicament in the beginning season. Instead of regrouping back to the principal actors, which was the agenda of the show, they discovered that the audience identified more with Michael J. Fox than the parents, Michael Gross and Meredith Baxter Berney. Although the comparison may not be germane, Parker and Danny always had great entrances and exits. The sum total of their lines in some episodes was, while making an entrance, saying "Hi"!

As the series ended, Parker was in the best position for his career. Represented by Harry Gold, Parker was billed as the best in his agency. This was a plus. There are a lot of jobs that would depend on whether or not the agent or manager would work hard for you. This status paid off, and Parker won a shot for five episodes of *The Wonder Years.* Parker got the job because the actor who played "Paul" broke his leg. The show was important for Parker, both as a job and for him personally. The actors cast on *Wonder Years* were all seasoned and had been around. Even for child actors, there were veterans who commanded much respect. Being cast on the show made Parker feel that he had "arrived" in some sense.

A lot of the small parts on the show were cast with good actors. Surrounded by such talent was stimulating and gave Parker a sense of accomplishment. For Parker, the famous "Big Stars" were not viewed as larger than life, at least that's what Parker felt. While eating lunch with the other actors on set, the star, Fred Savage, saw Shawn Cassidy walk by. Fred was in awe. This was puzzling and somewhat humorous to Parker, considering the status of Cassidy then compared to that of Savage at the time. Fame does carry an aura of inexplicable influence.

Parker's perspective was both individual and indicative of the experience of our family. In his own words:

> "What grounded me was my family background. You look at it at the surface and say that we didn't make it, but that's not all to the story.

> Some think that little Mormon kids are sheltered. Yet those who become stars in the industry are trying to find themselves with drugs and other indulgences. I've always been told not to do drugs, but until I saw others doing drugs I didn't know why. I now know how people get messed up. I've seen all the parties, with kids taking drugs, I definitely have a better perspective, which I accrued at a very young age. I had a support system, I had the safety of my family and the Church."

There was a price to pay and like the other children, he often judged his life by what others would deem as normal. Parker continues:

> "Sometimes I did get down. I missed out on a lot of Scouting and other school activities. I sacrificed a lot. I didn't have any after-school activities. But, to act together in our family was great! To be acting alongside of Christian was great because I like my brother. It was fun because we both liked acting. Once in a while I would stress out, and think maybe I'm not doing well. This occurred when I would have slow times, then I would get jobs very unexpectedly. On rare occasions I'd get jobs just on the first initial interview. This would result in the casting agent sending everybody else home."

One aspect of the industry which was a positive experience for Parker was the education he received as an actor, both on and off set, in school for three hours a day. One might think that such schools would be inadequate and a token effort. However, set schools were advantageous for Parker. The one-on-one teaching experience was invigorating. When Parker went back to public school, he was bored. The teacher would say, "He never looks at me," but he was use to the one on one. On set, he got strait A's with constant attention and individual education.

Without a competitive bone in his body, Parker left the industry when he turned 19. Like his brother and sister, he felt a need to give of himself in the service of his fellow human beings. Parker, volunteered for a mission. He was called to the West Virginia Charleston Mission in 1994.

The Family

On an August day in Provo in 1985, we looked at the majestic mountains and the blue, blue sky laced with whiter clouds than we ever saw in California. We knew of the cohesive neighborhood and community and peerless education system of the State of Utah and we asked, "Wouldn't this be a better place to rear our family?" The answer was, "yes!" So what effect would Hollywood's life style have upon us back in Utah?

And so some of us no longer live in California. And unfortunately, we are no longer a single, intact, family. Before the divorce we collectively decided to move back to Utah. Rebecca and I have both re-married and reside in the Salt Lake Valley. Rachel, Christian and Parker now have their own children. As a pleased father, may I give a complement to my children who have survived many pitfalls and have overcome many unusual obstacles and have grown strong through adversity.

One need not look too hard at the headlines to see the lives of Hollywood child actors who have hit hard times. Some, like our friend River Phoenix, didn't survive the effects of stardom. If the price of fame is desecration, sorrow, and misery, then I can be thankful that my children never achieved such worldly renown. I have a clean conscience about taking myself, my wife, and children to Hollywood and providing us all the opportunity to participant in these extraordinary experiences. Our particular story is one of success and blessings through obedience and hard work. My reward now comes by watching my children as they teach their children to make their own right choices and to stand triumphant in doing what our Heavenly Father would want them to do. They are examples of faith and accomplishment. Their worth cannot be measured by Nielsen Ratings or press reviews.

The foundation for our financial security was miraculously and painstakingly constructed in California. Our earthly riches and wealth are temporary, but our faith is eternal. For by our faith our fortune is not just now, but "He who hath Eternal Life is rich."

The End

References

Michael Medved, *Hollywood vs. America* (New York: Harper Perennial, 1992).

Printed in the United States
5496

10